Cinema and Surveillance

Cinema and Surveillance: The Asymmetric Gaze shows how key modern filmmakers challenge and disturb the relation between film and surveillance, medium and message. Assembling readings of films by Harun Farocki, Michael Haneke, and Fritz Lang, the book considers surveillance in such different domains as urban life, religious doctrine, and law enforcement.

With surveillance present in the modern world as both a technological phenomenon and a social practice, the author shows how cinema, as a visual medium, presents highly sophisticated analyses of surveillance. He suggests that "surveillance" is less an issue to be tackled from a secure spectatorial position than an experience to be rendered, an event to be dealt with. Far from offering a general model of spectatorship, the book explores how narrative moments of surveillance are complicated by specific spectatorial responses.

In its intersection of well-known figures and a highly topical issue, this book will have broad appeal, especially, but not exclusively, among students and scholars in film studies, media studies, German studies, European studies, art history, and political theory.

Martin Blumenthal-Barby is a Professor in the Department of Modern and Classical Literatures and Cultures at Rice University, where he also co-directs the Program in Cinema and Media Studies.

Routledge Focus on Film Studies

Robot Ecology and the Science Fiction Film
J. P. Telotte

Unproduction Studies and the American Film Industry
James Fenwick

Indian Indies
A Guide to New Independent Indian Cinema
Ashvin Immanuel Devasundaram

Migration and Identity in British East and Southeast Asian Cinema
Leung Wing-Fai

Con Artists in Cinema
Self-Knowledge, Female Power, and Love
Joseph H. Kupfer

The Body in Jean-Luc Godard's New Wave Films
Francesca Minnie Hardy

Jürgen Böttcher and Documentary Film
Documentaries, Contemporaries, History
Elizabeth Daggett Matar

Decolonial Imaginaries in Palestinian Experimental Film and Video
Postnational and Feminist Aesthetics
Kristin Lené Hole

Cinema and Surveillance
The Asymmetric Gaze
Martin Blumenthal-Barby

For more information about this series, please visit: https://www.routledge.com/Routledge-Focus-on-Film-Studies/book-series/RFFS

Cinema and Surveillance

The Asymmetric Gaze

By Martin Blumenthal-Barby

LONDON AND NEW YORK

First published 2024
by Routledge
4 Park Square, Milton Park, Abingdon, Oxon OX14 4RN

and by Routledge
605 Third Avenue, New York, NY 10158

Routledge is an imprint of the Taylor & Francis Group, an informa business

British Library Cataloguing-in-Publication Data
A catalogue record for this book is available from the British Library

Library of Congress Cataloging-in-Publication Data
Names: Blumenthal-Barby, Martin, author.
Title: Cinema and surveillance : the asymmetric gaze / by Martin Blumenthal-Barby.
Description: New York : Routledge, 2024. | Series: Routledge focus on film studies | Includes bibliographical references and index.
Identifiers: LCCN 2024015405 (print) | LCCN 2024015406 (ebook) | ISBN 9781032134611 (hardback) | ISBN 9781032135564 (paperback) | ISBN 9781003229834 (ebook)
Subjects: LCSH: Surveillance in motion pictures. | Motion pictures--Philosophy.
Classification: LCC PN1995.9.S86 B57 2024 (print) | LCC PN1995.9.S86 (ebook) | DDC 791.43/655--dc23/eng/20240403
LC record available at https://lccn.loc.gov/2024015405
LC ebook record available at https://lccn.loc.gov/2024015406

ISBN: 978-1-032-13461-1 (hbk)
ISBN: 978-1-032-13556-4 (pbk)
ISBN: 978-1-003-22983-4 (ebk)

DOI: 10.4324/9781003229834

Typeset in Times New Roman
by KnowledgeWorks Global Ltd.

"Martin Blumenthal-Barby offers a succinct yet profound analysis of the complex dynamics involved in surveillance. With insightful readings of three canonical artists—Harun Farocki, Michael Haneke, and Fritz Lang—Blumenthal-Barby shows how we as viewers become implicated in complex image economies and asymmetrical relations between observer and observed. Reading closely with Blumenthal-Barby, we come to participate in the power dynamics of the surveillant works he discusses. Ever so rarely, as he lucidly shows, we undermine those dynamics through our very participation."

Fatima Naqvi, *Elias W. Leavenworth Professor of Germanic Languages and Literatures & Film and Media Studies, Yale University*

"This elegant, compact book performs an exercise in close looking—at the ways in which we are always being watched. Its careful tracing of the surveillant in three major works asks us to reckon with cinema as an ontologically guilty medium."

John David Rhodes, *University of Cambridge*

"Martin Blumenthal-Barby's *Cinema and Surveillance* is a work of singular importance in our media-saturated age where surveillance cameras and satellites are ubiquitous. With a delicate hand, Blumenthal-Barby shows how experimental cinema unmasks the position of the observer otherwise hidden from sight and explores the ethical implications of a distant gaze that participates in the violence that it records. The book masterfully orchestrates a dialogue between thinkers as varied as Jeremy Bentham, Hans Blumenberg, Michel Foucault, and Georg Simmel and the filmmakers Harun Farocki, Michael Haneke, and Fritz Lang. *Cinema and Surveillance* is essential reading for anyone concerned about the powers of the state and the possibilities for film in our political climate."

Rochelle Tobias, *Johns Hopkins University*

"Martin Blumenthal-Barby's *Cinema and Surveillance* deserves to be read widely, both by those who study surveillance and those interested in the cinema more broadly. Unlike many who work on this topic, Blumenthal-Barby writes with great lucidity, and he penetrates to the core of complex theoretical arguments precisely and concisely. The book is therefore an excellent primer for those new to the field of surveillance studies. But Blumenthal-Barby does more by offering sophisticated and illuminating readings of works by Farocki, Haneke, and Lang in the context of theories of surveillance. He thereby reveals aspects of their work I, for one, had not considered before and makes a genuine contribution to the study of these major filmmakers."

Malcolm Turvey, *Sol Gittleman Professor, Tufts University*

"In *Cinema and Surveillance*, Martin Blumenthal-Barby pushes theories of spectatorship and voyeuristic pleasure beyond the entrenched paradigms we have inherited. In stunning readings of films by Harun Farocki, Michael Haneke, and Fritz Lang, Blumenthal-Barby demonstrates that surveillance is not always, or perforce, an experience of visual mastery. It is, above all, a performance that the viewer takes part in through discrete aesthetic strategies, which give rise to feelings of discomfort, implication, and exposure. Reading this concise and inventive book, I come to the uneasy revelation that these films are also watching me."

Jennifer Fay, *Gertrude Conaway Vanderbilt Professor of Cinema & Media Arts, Vanderbilt University*

"It has become a commonplace of media theory to regard the culture of surveillance, which is often said to emerge in the twentieth century with the advent of moving image technologies, as an overwhelming effect of those technologies—as if free will and human flourishing would have continued unabated were it not for the camera. Beginning with the Old Testament, where others might begin with the Bolex, Blumenthal-Barby's ground-breaking new book, *Cinema and Surveillance*, guides us toward a more complex understanding of technology, toward the ways that cinema complicates the relation between seeing and being seen, which moves always in more than one direction. It is a stunning description of both how much deeper, how much older, the problem of being watched is and a brilliant account of how cinema helps us to think critically and agentially from within a control society facilitated by the camera, even though the camera is but the latest tool in the longstanding work of moral, social, and economic coordination."

Brian Price, *University of Toronto*

"Blumenthal-Barby constructs a compelling narrative for explaining Harun Farocki's 'Counter-Music,' a multifaceted installation with many visual scenes and inputs (from traffic light patterns to electricity grids and mobile phone networks). In addressing such a complex work in a fashion accessible to students of Cultural Studies and literature, Blumenthal-Barby continues in the footsteps of the trend-setting comparatist Eduardo Cadava (Princeton), who has made the full-service theoretical 'turn to the visual' before him. Blumenthal-Barby succeeds as a theoretically-oriented close reader who renders authoritative exegeses of exemplary artifacts."

Henry Sussman, *Yale University*

Contents

Acknowledgments

This little book was disturbingly long in the making. I must thank the various colleagues and friends who have patiently listened to my thoughts on cinema and surveillance and shared their own over the better part of the last decade. During the project's inception at the Stanford Humanities Center, I greatly benefited from conversations with Malcolm Turvey, Amir Eshel, Russell Berman, Namwali Serpell, Adrian Daub, and Peggy Phelan. In the subsequent years, I found an intellectual haven and discerning interlocutors at the annual World Picture Conference, above all, Brian Price, John David Rhodes, Meghan Sutherland, Eugenie Brinkema, and Jessica Ruffin. Henry Sussman, Jaimey Fisher, Rochelle Tobias, Geoffrey Winthrop-Young, Ansgar Mohnkern, Karin Bauer, Betiel Wasihun, Todd Herzog, Leif Weatherby, and Anton Kaes offered shrewd feedback and nuanced insights along the way. Harriet Bergmann and Marian Rogers graciously aided in copyediting the manuscript. Suzanne Richardson at Routledge oversaw the review and production process with wonderful professionalism. My family in the New World and the Old World provided stimulating input and welcome distractions that made it all worthwhile. No doubt, I owe most of my thinking about cinema and surveillance to the productive challenges and inspiring curiosity of my students, and thus, I dedicate this book to them.

Introduction

We live in an age of surveillance.[1] Surveillance is with us both as a technological phenomenon and as a social practice. While some of the most salient categories of modern life, such as the distinction between private and public, individual and collective, man and machine, reality and fiction, appear inextricably linked to questions of surveillance, it seems safe to say that surveillance as such, directly and unequivocally, has emerged as a major player in the modern age. Martin Heidegger, in a 1938 lecture, suggested that we live in "the age of the world picture," by which he did not mean "a picture of the world" but rather "the world conceived and grasped as picture." This propensity to conceive and grasp the world as a picture serves, according to Heidegger, "*man's making himself secure* as subiectum," his "self-establishing within the world as picture." He emphasized, "Wherever we have the world picture, an essential decision takes place regarding what is, in its entirety."[2] In line with Heidegger's claim that we live in "the age of the world picture," it appears appropriate, this book will suggest, to advance the corresponding claim that we live in an age of surveillance.

I

To be sure, many of the most perceptive critical thinkers of recent decades have remarked on this ever more present force of surveillance and, in different ways and under different names, put forth reflections on surveillance as part of their theoretical projects. In this context, some thinkers, more or less explicitly, have proven to be particularly influential in establishing theorems that have determined the field of surveillance studies and, at times, narrowed its scope. In the following pages, I shall cursorily outline the most important of these theoretical positions so as to, on the one hand, elucidate their terminological breadth, and, on the other hand, contextualize some of the recurring metaphors and concepts they have developed on surveillance, metaphors and concepts that will also emerge from this book.

DOI: 10.4324/9781003229834-1

The Old and the New Testaments are perhaps the groundbreaking treatises on surveillance, specifically with regard to their repeated characterization of God's gaze as all-seeing and omniscient. "Neither is there any creature that is not manifest in his sight: but all things are naked and opened unto the eyes of him with whom we have to do," Hebrews 4:13 reads, a verse for which many an equivalent could be provided. We will, in the course of this book, frequently refer to this biblical notion of surveillance, sometimes directly and at other times by way of its secular manifestation, that is, by way of what Friedrich Schiller famously described in his "The Song of the Bell" as the vigilant "eye of the law."[3] Yet even without going that far back in time, one is likely to encounter representatives of different academic disciplines who have concerned themselves with surveillance, or rather with certain facets of and phenomena contiguous to surveillance. A prominent representative, if we begin in the early twentieth century, is the German sociologist Max Weber, whose thoughts on the matter of bureaucracy mark a central constituent of modern societies' control mechanisms. Weber understood the extent to which bureaucratic record-keeping, understood here as "file-based surveillance,"[4] permeates and regulates modern societies, and how much its underlying principle of rationalization depends on its being conceived as antipode to human beings, that is to say, how much it relies on "dehumanization":

> When fully developed, bureaucracy [...] stands [...] under the principle of *sine ira ac studio*. Bureaucracy develops the more perfectly, the more it is "dehumanized," the more completely it succeeds in eliminating from official business love, hatred, and all purely personal, irrational and emotional elements which escape calculation.[5]

While the Bible, most famously in the book of Numbers (1–4, 26), already tells of a census and as such provides an instance of file-based surveillance, it was Weber who understood and theorized the encompassing and pervasive force of bureaucratic control mechanisms for modern societies.

A contemporary of Weber, the sociologist Georg Simmel proves to be a source for an investigation into surveillance from a quite different angle, especially if one considers Simmel's thoughts on the significance of the look and the importance of "mutual glances."[6] His thoughts shed light, obliquely, on the fundamental *discrepancy*, the radical *asymmetry* that appears to characterize most surveillance and, as such, figures as a sort of leitmotif in this book. While surveillance typically implies a certain imbalance, the asymmetrical situation of "seeing without being seen,"[7] Simmel stresses how much the human glance is configured in terms of an interrelationality "between eye and eye,"[8] and, if we extrapolate, what a harmful interference surveillance constitutes for a presumably natural economy of interpersonal perception. "This highest psychic reaction [...] in which the glances of eye to eye unite men [...] dies in the moment in which the immediacy of the function is lost."

"[I]n distinction from the [...] observation of the other," Simmel emphasizes, the "glances of eye to eye" denote a particularly pure "interaction," because "[by] the glance which reveals the other, one discloses oneself. [...] The eye cannot take unless at the same time it gives."[9] The interrelationality inscribed into the exchange of glances leads Simmel to claim that the interpersonal exchange of glances exemplifies "the most perfect reciprocity in the entire field of human relationships."[10]

How vulnerable the reciprocity so emphatically asserted here really is becomes painfully clear in Jean-Paul Sartre's description of the voyeur staring through a keyhole in *Being and Nothingness* (1943).[11] Departing from the question "What does *being seen* mean for me?" Sartre asks us to imagine that "moved by jealousy, curiosity, or vice" he, Sartre, eavesdrops at a door and peeks through its keyhole: "I am alone and on the level of a non-thetic self-consciousness," meaning "there is no self to inhabit my consciousness [...]. My consciousness sticks to my acts, it *is* my acts." "But all of a sudden I hear footsteps in the hall," he continues.

> Someone is looking at me! What does this mean? It means that I am suddenly affected in my being and that essential modifications appear in my structure—modifications which I can apprehend and fix conceptually by means of the reflective *cogito*. [...] [A]ll of a sudden I am conscious of myself [...] in that I have my foundation outside myself. [...] It is shame [...] which reveals to me the Other's look and myself at the end of that look.[12]

It would be too much here to attempt a detailed analysis of the scene sketched by Sartre.[13] As can be gleaned from the lines succeeding the scene, it is heavily inspired by Hegel's famous lord-bondsman dialectic, with Sartre's putatively dominant voyeur abruptly gaining consciousness of himself as someone who not only sees but is also seen, who develops a sense of his being, his personhood, specifically from this *re*-flective self-conception and thus puts himself into "slavish" dependence on the other, or rather on *the look* of the other. Against the backdrop of Simmel's analysis of (symmetric) seeing and being seen, Sartre introduces a number of categories here that are relevant to the question of surveillance,[14] and, as such, will surface in one way or another in the chapters of this book: first, (in its asymmetry) the *antagonistic* relation between observer and observed, between surveillor and surveilled;[15] second, the differentiation between the look and the eye,[16] whereby a look, curiously, is experienced as particularly powerful when the eye or the person who looks remains unseen;[17] finally, the effect of the look upon the constitution of personhood, upon the mental state of a person and specifically the evocation of "shame."[18]

It goes without saying that a particularly influential text for the study of surveillance is Michel Foucault's 1975 *Discipline and Punish*, specifically in terms of the model of the panopticon it problematizes. Of course, Foucault encountered this model in the letters of the English utilitarian philosopher Jeremy Bentham. Bentham developed the architecture of the panopticon specifically with an eye to the efficacy of prisons, yet he deemed it applicable to other domains of society as well, including schools, hospitals, and manufactories, among others. The model of the panopticon was based on the idea of an *asymmetrical* economy of gazes, of a "seeing without being seen,"[19] which, in our context, will be considered to constitute the core of all surveillance. The prison was structured as a circle with a tower at its center, the "*inspector's lodge*,"[20] from which the guard could look into the inmates' cells placed along the periphery. The panopticon's architecture allowed for a controlled channeling of light and looks, so that the watchman could see the inmates, yet the inmates could not see the watchman. Even though it was perfectly clear that the watchman could never observe all inmates at once, the inmates still felt incessantly observed because they might be observed at any given moment. Bentham writes, "[T]he persons to be inspected should always feel themselves as if under inspection": "[T]he greater chance there is, of a given person's being at a given time actually under inspection, the more strong will be the persuasion—the more *intense* [...] the *feeling*, he has of his being so."[21] The gist of Bentham's idea consisted in the translation of an architectural configuration into a psychological conditioning.[22] Some two hundred years later, Foucault (who figures especially in Chapters 2 and 3 of this book) takes up the functioning of the panopticon and declares it, based on his abstracting and delimiting reading, to be the paradigmatic model of so-called disciplinary societies characteristic of the eighteenth and nineteenth centuries. "[O]ne can speak of the formation of a disciplinary society," Foucault notes, "that stretches from the enclosed disciplines, a sort of social 'quarantine,' to an indefinitely generalizable mechanism of 'panopticism.'"[23] Foucault is less interested in a specific architectural configuration than the "generalizable" dynamic[24] that Bentham's prison model and its asymmetric economy of gazes ("seeing without being seen") seemed to generate.[25] This is a mechanism that (albeit fundamentally called into question in Chapter 3) rests upon the putative observation of the guards and the resultant appropriation of behavioral codes through the inmates. Foucault, in other words, is interested in a dynamic according to which bodies are formed into "docile bodies,"[26] not based on punitive violence or actual surveillance, but on the efficacy of internalization, that is, the effective conjuring up of the *appearance* of surveillance and the corresponding conditioning of human beings.[27] The Foucauldian conception of "panopticism" is, due to its explanatory force, certainly the model that has most profoundly shaped the field of surveillance studies, even if, due to its monopolistic status, not always for the better.

Of the many critics who have grappled with Foucault's theoretical provocations and taken him as a point of departure for their own thinking, perhaps the most prominent example is Gilles Deleuze (who plays an explicit role in

Chapter 1).[28] In a short yet dense essay entitled "Postscript on the Societies of Control," Deleuze observes a move away from "disciplinary societies," as Foucault had postulated them, toward so-called societies of control. Deleuze reminds us that Foucault situates disciplinary societies in the period from the eighteenth to the early twentieth century, their pivotal characteristic being "vast spaces of enclosure": "The individual never ceases passing from one closed environment to another, each having its own laws: first, the family; then the school [...] then the barracks [...] then the factory; from time to time the hospital; possibly the prison, the preeminent instance of the enclosed environment."[29] To be sure, Deleuze acknowledges the explanatory force of Foucault's analysis, yet he identifies a general "crisis in relation to all the environments of enclosure"[30] for the second half of the twentieth century, largely due to the increasing computerization of modern life and the concomitant emergence of what he calls "societies of control." "In the disciplinary societies," he writes,

> one was always starting again (from school to the barracks, from the barracks to the factory), while in the societies of control one is never finished with anything—the corporation, the educational system, the armed services being metastable states coexisting in one and the same modulation, like a universal system of deformation.[31]

The implications that these "societies of control" have for the very defining of "human beings" are fundamental, as will become apparent in Chapter 1. At one of the essay's conceptually clearest moments, Deleuze distinguishes the (spatially and temporally) fixed nature of *enclosures* from the much more elusive (albeit no less pervasive) *controls*: he characterizes the former as "molds" and the latter as "modulations," thus hinting at the rapidly changing, ever transforming logic of societies of control.[32]

The "new system of domination" described by Deleuze reverberates, as he himself recognized, with Paul Virilio's approach to the issues of surveillance and control,[33] most emphatically articulated in Virilio's 1988 *Vision Machine*. Virilio (who figures in Chapter 1) concerns himself with vision machines, which, as a result of the algorithmic processing of the field of vision, analyze and interpret events, bringing about a sort of "*automation of perception*," or, indeed, "the innovation of artificial vision."[34] While these vision machines find their primary application in military operations and industrial production, they increasingly infiltrate everyday life by way of so-called intelligent surveillance cameras.[35] Virilio writes,

> Whence the sudden welter of instantaneous retransmission equipment, in town, in the office, at home: all this real-time TV monitoring tirelessly on the lookout for the unexpected, the impromptu, whatever might suddenly crop up, anywhere, any day, at the bank, the supermarket, the sports

> ground where the video referee has not long taken over from the referee on the field.[36]

Vision machines, according to Virilio, are part of an "industrialisation of prevention, or prediction: a sort of panic anticipation," which will "rule out the surprise, the accident, the irruption of the unforeseen," that is, all that which, in the purview of a particular surveilled system, must be considered nonsystemic.[37] Control appears to be enforced here in seemingly "soft" and imperceptible ways, yet is, in view of the massive proliferation of these surveillance systems, no less effective than the enclosed systems that Foucault deemed characteristic of disciplinary societies.

Although much less frequently discussed in surveillance studies than, say, Foucault, the work of Jacques Lacan, specifically his influential theorization of the gaze, must be noticed here. Of course, Lacan explicitly concerns himself with the aforementioned scene of voyeurism from Sartre's *Being and Nothingness*. "The gaze, as conceived by Sartre," he notes, "is the gaze by which I am surprised [...]. In so far as I am under the gaze, Sartre writes, I no longer see the eye that looks at me and, if I see the eye, the gaze disappears. [...] The gaze I encounter [...] is not a seen gaze, but a gaze imagined by me in the field of the Other."[38] While all this seems to be in line with our earlier discussion, Lacan importantly points out:

> If you turn to Sartre's [...] text, you will see that, far from speaking of the emergence of this gaze as of something that concerns the organ of sight, he refers to the sound of rustling leaves, suddenly heard while out hunting, to a footstep heard in a corridor. And when are these sounds heard? At the moment when he has presented himself in the action of looking through a keyhole.[39]

The gaze that surprises the voyeur is, according to Lacan, a gaze that is not only "not [...] seen" but, indeed, a gaze that is perceived on the basis of *sound*. It pertains not to "the organ of sight" but is experienced as a result of sonic stimuli.[40] While Lacan's considerations of the gaze could at least obliquely be developed toward a theory of surveillance (a possible point of departure would be his remarks on the "mirror stage"[41]), one if not *the* most influential Lacanian of recent decades, Slavoj Žižek, has addressed the subject of surveillance directly. In an essay entitled "Big Brother, or, the Triumph of the Gaze over the Eye," Žižek ponders the enormous popularity of current-day reality TV shows and observes a "tragic-comic reversal of the Bentham-Orwellian notion of the Panopticon-society," which prompted the sense of permanently being observed and of having "no place to hide from the omnipresent gaze of the Power." By contrast, today, he argues, "anxiety seems to arise from the prospect of NOT being exposed to the Other's gaze all the time" and the subject's need for "the camera's gaze as a kind of ontological guarantee of his/her being."[42] What we are dealing with here is (among the instances considered in this book) but one example of a curious inversion of the Benthamite conception of a powerful observer and a disempowered observed in favor of an observed who feels empowered, who, in Žižek's case, indeed seizes his or her very sense of existence from being subjected to an Other's gaze.

In addition to all these thinkers who, to a greater or lesser extent, have been considered in the critical literature on surveillance and who, to a greater or lesser extent, will make an appearance in the subsequent chapters, there are names that thus far have hardly attracted interest in surveillance studies, even though they seem to hold great potential for an investigation of surveillance. A case in point is the German philosopher Hans Blumenberg, who, in his 1979 *Shipwreck with Spectator*, seeks to explore the paradigmatic case of a "metaphor for existence" (*Daseinsmetapher*). Surveying the history of Western literature and philosophy from antiquity to the twentieth century, Blumenberg explores the metaphor "shipwreck with spectator," which initially involves a spectator "observing [...] other people who are in peril on the storm-tossed sea" from the safety of dry land.[43] Blumenberg explains that the "spectacle of confusion and wreckage" out in the sea captivates spectators, as they can "smugly look on at the distant spectacle" from "the solid ground of the shore."[44] He is eager to point out that it typically is less "complacency" that we experience when observing the misery of those who suffer shipwreck and drown than the gradual realization of how much our "secure position" as "unimperiled" observers is owed to "good fortune."[45] And yet the view from solid ground onto the sea—into the "sphere of the unreckonable and lawless, [...] [of] evil [...], of the arbitrariness of the powers" and the shipwrecked struggling for their lives (metaphorizing people's struggle with the hardships of reality)—is, after all, never entirely free of the "secret" spectatorial pleasure so frequently experienced by those performing an act of surveillance.[46]

Another example of a thinker whose work has been drawn on surprisingly little in discussions of surveillance is the sociologist Niklas Luhmann. One of the key concepts in Luhmann's influential systems theory is, of course, "observation." Luhmann explains that he uses the term in the most abstract sense and "independently of [...] the specific mode of operation that enable[s] observations to be carried out." Beyond the visual connotation typically associated with the term, for Luhmann, "observing means simply distinguishing and indicating."[47] To be sure, the act of observation raises the question of who observes the observer, and here Luhmann introduces his conception of second-order observation. A second-order observer is someone who "refers to an observer of the first order and [...] distinguishes and indicates an observation as observation."[48] While second-order observation can denote the observation of others as observers, it can also imply the observation of oneself as an observer, in which case we would encounter a form of self-observation.[49] Here, then, Luhmann's concerns appear germane to our discussion of surveillance. "[T]here may be a link," he writes,

> between the possibility for self-observation, on the one hand, and of second-order observation of others, on the other. If one can see others as observers, then why not oneself, too? […] Individuals are self-observers. They become individuals by observing their own observations. Today, they are no longer defined by birth, by social origin, or by characteristics that distinguish them from all other individuals. […] One might argue with Simmel […] or Sartre that they acquire their identity through the gaze of others, but only on condition that they observe that they are being observed.[50]

What matters here for our purposes is Luhmann's proposition that the constitution of identity may well be contingent upon "the gaze of others" (which he notes has been suggested by Simmel and Sartre), yet "only on condition" of one's self-observation or, we might say, one's self-monitoring. Beyond the explicit references to Simmel and Sartre, beyond distinct contiguities with Foucault and Blumenberg, to name but a few, we can certainly add Luhmann to our discussion of theorists whose work speaks to the issue of surveillance.

II

Because through their theoretical approaches the aforementioned thinkers have a great deal to say about our topic, we will, in the course of this book, engage in a dialogue with some of them and encounter others as critical interlocutors. At the same time, however, surveillance is often a *visual* phenomenon. It describes some sort of "watch […] kept over a person, etc., esp. over a suspected person, a prisoner, or the like."[51] Because of the decidedly visual efficacy of much surveillance, it is hardly surprising that visual works—and specifically cinematic works of art—have provided particularly sophisticated analyses of surveillance. What is striking is that surveillance does not merely figure in filmic works that tackle the issue head-on and make it the center of thematic investigation. Surveillance emerges, tacitly yet persistently, seemingly everywhere, and that indeed is one of the core claims of this book.

This book assembles readings of films that consider surveillance in such different domains as urban life, religious doctrine, and law enforcement. Yet it is not merely their ostensible engagement with surveillance that makes the films in question so receptive to an investigation into surveillance. To be sure, each of the films dealt with in this book addresses surveillance directly and emphatically and has a lot to say *about* surveillance. Harun Farocki's installation *Counter-Music* (Chapter 1) unambiguously addresses the use of surveillance technologies in modern cities. Similarly, Michael Haneke's celebrated film *Caché* (Chapter 2) and Fritz Lang's classic *M* (Chapter 3) forcefully take up the issue of surveillance. And yet, even though surveillance appears to be at the center of the works explored in this book, it emerges with such insistence one wonders how much of the ubiquity of surveillance is due to an affinity with the cinematic medium and cinematic spectatorship itself. One indeed might feel inclined to ask how much the putatively voyeuristic act of watching film in a darkness that does not allow for a gaze in return enacts the basic asymmetrical situation of surveillance, whose dynamic, in one way or another, is always that of a seeing without being seen.

But before we begin applying some sort of theoretical model to the radically different films in question, we should pause and ask what kinds of films we are actually dealing with here, what questions they raise, and what enactments they offer. Farocki's 2004 *Counter-Music*, a twenty-three-minute-long installation discussed in Chapter 1, is, at first sight, a city film in the tradition of Walter Ruttmann's *Berlin: Symphony of a Great City* (1927) and Dziga Vertov's *The Man with the Movie Camera* (1929). In contrast to these classic city symphony films from the early twentieth century that Farocki repeatedly cites, his installation consists less of newly shot footage of a city (in his case, the French city of Lille) than of images that already exist as an integral part of the city. Farocki presents his city film through images shot by surveillance cameras, images that he, in turn, merely arranges. Yet it is precisely the kind of arrangement, his style of montage, and the mode of spectatorship his style induces that account for the specificity of his film. While Farocki documents the life of a city that increasingly relies on automatic surveillance systems for regulation, thereby alluding to the *expulsion* of human viewers, Farocki's installation, specifically his complex split-screen aesthetics, depends on the *involvement* of human spectators and their ability to reflect. While the core of *Counter-Music* is made up of so-called operational images, which are not meant to be viewed by human beings but by computers equipped with automatic recognition software, Farocki's complex "soft montage" technique relies heavily on human recipients, their creative input, and their readiness to interpret his work. Farocki, as it were, performatively undoes the very dynamic that he describes constatively: The asserted abolition of the work of the eye through automated surveillance systems is unsettled by his art of montage and the mode of reception it provokes with its reliance upon imaginative (rather than automatized) readers.

Certainly, some form of such peculiar interplay between subject matter and presentational manner permeates Chapter 2, which examines Michael Haneke's *Caché* (2005). Yet the exact nature of this interplay is quite different from Farocki's, especially with respect to the issue of surveillance. The interplay between thematic matter and aesthetic manner specifically results in a quite different "enactment" or "performance" of surveillance, which, throughout the book, indeed, presents itself less as a matter to be examined from a beholder's viewpoint than an experience to be appropriated, to be dealt with, and, at times, to be suffered by us as cinematic spectators. Haneke's film *Caché* has drawn more critical attention than most in recent film history. Many of these studies have, with good reason, focused on the theme of guilt, which permeates much of Haneke's oeuvre and figures prominently in *Caché*. Surprisingly few discussions have tackled the conspicuous presence of surveillance in the film, which we encounter right at its beginning and which, one might argue, permeates the film to the last scene. Chapter 2 focuses on surveillance and argues that Haneke's utterly mysterious film lends itself to a reading that relates the issues of guilt and surveillance, conceiving of guilt as enmeshed with surveillance, and surveillance as inextricably linked with the notion of guilt. Thus, Haneke's film confronts viewers with, and implicates them in, a quasi-religious experience that seems absent in much contemporary surveillance discourse but in fact lies at its core.

If the film's first shot initially appears as filmic narrative and only subsequently presents itself as a film within the film, as surveillance tape watched by diegetic characters, then this clearly marked separation between Haneke's film and surveillance tapes within the film's diegesis appears increasingly hard to make out, so much so that the enigmatic final shot echoes the film's first shot in cinematography (long take, wide static frame) while lacking any concrete indication of its being or not being surveillance footage. Importantly, Haneke's destabilization of mediatic boundaries—between diegetic surveillance tapes and filmic narrative—involves us as spectators who, like the film's protagonist, watch these images, and who, just like Georges, are called upon, indeed pressed, to respond and to conjure up a sense of responsibility to that history of colonial violence in which we most likely participate, not directly as agents but perhaps as accomplices. What emerges is Haneke's view that we all live in a state of guilt, his characters as much as we, his spectators, and it is incumbent on us to account for this guilt and respond to it. *Caché* is surveillance cinema conceived at a time of ubiquitous surveillance that forces us back into the experience of guilt-ridden subjects observed and self-observing in light of the power-political atrocities we are embroiled in and entangled with. While the protagonist, Georges, does not acknowledge this entanglement and ensuing responsibility, Haneke's film provides an imaginative space in which to experience and account for a reality that is ours to reckon with.

While Chapter 2 investigates surveillance against the backdrop of the question of the divine, Chapter 3 considers surveillance with reference to the notion of the diabolic. The final chapter takes up Fritz Lang's classic 1931 film *M*, which centers on the sinister serial killer and child murderer Hans Beckert, who has thrust the city into a state of crisis. This society, with its manifold disciplinary structures, sets out to guarantee the safety of the children, yet *fails* to do precisely that, again and again. In the wake of the failed panoptic surveillance, the child murderer drives the city into an atmospheric state of exception. Not only the police but the entire city is urged to locate the child murderer, who has affected social life to the point where all norms and usual procedures are suspended, and thus must be tracked down. What conceptually emerges is a transition from *panoptic* to *synoptic* surveillance—that is, we are no longer dealing with the surveillance of *many* by *one* (in Benthamite terms, of *many* prisoners by *one* guard), but increasingly with the surveillance of *one* person by *many* people. The entire urban population is frantically searching for the child murderer. Symptomatic of this synoptic state of surveillance, the tracking and monitoring of the *one*, the child murderer, by the *many*, the mob, gives rise to an all-encompassing sense of distrust, a climate of categorical suspicion, that paralyzes communal life. In describing this transition from institutions to networks topologically, one might speak of a shift from a *vertical* structure (the prison guards who monitor the inmates) to a *horizontal* design. The vertical system is increasingly replaced by a flat formation in which there is no longer a concentric consolidation of power directed at subordinate subjects or "docile bodies," as Foucault described institutions in disciplinary societies. Instead, we are dealing with a network architecture in which everyone is involved, where control is both carried out and experienced by everyone: everyone is watcher and watched at the same time.

Curiously, surveillance takes place not only on a diegetic level; surveillance is not merely a matter of the police or the gangsters and their recruits, the beggars. Lang's camera itself is *surveillant* in various ways. At times, we witness the typical affectless camera gaze that nowadays is associated with automated camera surveillance and that indifferently records events or objects. Next to these affectless and matter-of-fact shots, testifying to the film's New Objectivity inflection, we encounter moments in which a (at times shaky) camera appears prying, inquisitive, displaying a curiosity that seems strangely furtive. What is more, in our role as spectators we are unremittingly implicated in the experience of surveillance. That is, the dynamic of seeing without being seen is unmistakably enacted by the camera and allows us to perceive surveillance as something not solely conceptually posited but indeed performed. And importantly, this performance or enactment emphatically involves us, in that we, perforce, must participate in the experience of surveillance. In other words, again we encounter that allegorical enactment of surveillance in which surveillance is not merely asserted thematically but rather conjured up as an experience in which we participate.

To be sure, while the films considered in this book are suited to elucidating various aspects of surveillance, none of the films discussed is merely a film *about* surveillance. *Counter-Music* is a city film in the tradition of Ruttmann and Vertov. *Caché* deals with an upper-middle-class French family and, more broadly, with the denial of individual and collective guilt. *M* is a film about the social chaos in Weimar Germany in the wake of World War I and during the Great Depression. In spite of the variety of purported themes, surveillance arises as epistemic register again and again and, significantly, does so in ways that insistently implicate us, the audience. If anything links the various readings performed in this book, it is specifically that "surveillance," over and over, appears less an issue to be tackled from some secure spectatorial position than an experience to be rendered, an event to be dealt with. Rather than merely serving as placeholder for cinematic spectatorship *as such*, surveillance repeatedly presents itself in terms of the enactment of particular narrative moments and the corresponding positioning of the viewer. Again and again, the question arises of how exactly the position of spectatorship relates to or is shaped by the negotiated issues of surveillance—whether by way of the split-screen aesthetics of "soft montage" (in the case of Farocki), through mediatic ambiguities and protracted long takes (Haneke), or via prying overhead shots and clandestine tracking shot arrangements (Lang). Far from offering a general model of spectatorship, this book investigates how narrative moments of surveillance are challenged and disturbed by specific spectatorial responses, and it is these moments of challenge and disturbance to which we shall now turn.

Notes

1 This book is based on my German monograph *Der asymmetrische Blick: Film und Überwachung* (Paderborn: Fink, 2016), though it differs substantially. I have adopted the introduction (with significant modifications) and an abbreviated version of chapter 1, which previously also appeared as "*Counter-Music*: Harun Farocki's Theory of a New Image Type" in *October* 151 (2015), published by MIT Press. Chapters 2 and 3 were newly written for this English-language edition with Routledge.
2 Martin Heidegger, *The Question Concerning Technology and Other Essays*, trans. William Lovitt (New York: Harper & Row, 1977), 115–54, here 129–30, 142, emphasis mine; Martin Heidegger, *Holzwege* (Frankfurt/M: Klostermann, 1977), 75–114, here 89–90, 101–2.
3 On the metaphoricity of the "eye of the law," see Michael Stolleis, *Das Auge des Gesetzes: Geschichte einer Metapher* (Munich: Verlag C. H. Beck, 2004), here especially 7–14.
4 David Lyon, *Surveillance Studies: An Overview* (Cambridge: Polity Press, 2007), 79; see also Christopher Dandeker, *Surveillance, Power and Modernity: Bureaucracy and Discipline from 1700 to the Present Day* (Cambridge: Polity Press, 1990).
5 Max Weber, *Economy and Society: An Outline of Interpretive Sociology* (Berkeley: University of California Press, 1978), 975.
6 Georg Simmel, *Soziologie: Untersuchungen über die Formen der Vergesellschaftung* (Berlin: Duncker & Humblot, 1908), 647. (Whenever possible, I have drawn on the translation provided in Georg Simmel, "Sociology of the Senses: Visual Interaction," in *Introduction to the Science of Sociology*, ed. R. E. Park and W. W. Burgess [Chicago: University of Chicago Press, 1969], 356–61. All other translations of Simmel are my own.) I am indebted here to the more elaborate discussions of Simmel's "sociology of the senses" by Dietmar Kammerer, *Bilder der Überwachung* (Frankfurt/M: Suhrkamp, 2008), 106–7, and Deena Weinstein and Michael Weinstein, "On the Visual Constitution of Society: The Contributions of Georg Simmel and Jean-Paul Sartre to a Sociology of the Senses," *History of European Ideas* 5.4 (1984): 349–62, here 349–55.
7 See notes 19 and 25.
8 Simmel, *Soziologie*, 653.

9 Simmel, *Soziologie*, 647–48.
10 Simmel, *Soziologie*, 648.
11 Various critics have drawn attention to the dissimilitude between Sartre's and Simmel's theorization of visual senses. See, among others, Weinstein and Weinstein, "On the Visual Constitution of Society," 349–62; Astrit Schmidt-Burkhardt, "The All-Seer: God's Eye as Proto-Surveillance," in *Ctrl Space: Rhetorics of Surveillance from Bentham to Big Brother*, ed. Thomas Levin, Ursula Frohne, and Peter Weibel (Cambridge, MA: MIT Press, 2002), 17–31, here 18n18; Janne Seppänen, *The Power of the Gaze: An Introduction to Visual Literacy* (New York: Peter Lang International Academic Publishers, 2006), 70. My discussion is indebted to the detailed analysis provided by Kammerer, *Bilder der Überwachung*, 107–10.
12 Jean-Paul Sartre, *Being and Nothingness: An Essay on Phenomenological Ontology* (London: Routledge, 2003), 282–85.
13 For insightful meditations, see Gregor Schwering, "Über das Auge triumphiert der Blick: Perspektiven des Voyerismus," in *Big Brother: Beobachtungen*, ed. Friedrich Balke, Gregor Schwering, and Urs Stäheli (Bielefeld: Transcript Verlag, 2000), 129–50, here especially 135–37; and Martin Jay, *Downcast Eyes: The Denigration of Vision in Twentieth-Century French Thought* (Berkeley: University of California Press, 1993), 287–92.
14 See Kammerer, *Bilder der Überwachung*, 109–10; and Weinstein and Weinstein, "On the Visual Constitution of Society."
15 Sartre, *Being and Nothingness*, 288. On this antagonism, see especially Jay, who convincingly stresses the emotively charged nature of the struggle when he identifies in Sartre a "hostile contest of wills between competing subjects" (*Downcast Eyes*, 287).
16 Sartre, *Being and Nothingness*, 282. Regarding the antagonistic relation between observer and observed, the differentiation between look and eye, and the question of how specifically the one interrelates with the other, see Kammerer, *Bilder der Überwachung*, 109–10, and Jay, *Downcast Eyes*, 287–88. My discussion is indebted to both critics' more elaborate analyses.
17 "[M]y apprehension of a look turned toward me appears on the ground of the destruction of the eyes which 'look at me.' [...] [T]he Other's look hides his eyes; it seems to *go in front of them*" (Sartre, *Being and Nothingness*, 282).
18 Sartre, *Being and Nothingness*, 284–86.
19 Jeremy Bentham, *The Panopticon Writings* (London: Verso, 1995), 43. On the asymmetry of gazes, see also David Lyon, *The Electronic Eye: The Rise of Surveillance Society* (Cambridge: Polity, 1994), 65.
20 Bentham, *The Panopticon Writings*, 35.
21 Bentham, *The Panopticon Writings*, 43–44.
22 Bentham, *The Panopticon Writings*, 31; see also David Rosen and Aaron Santesso, *The Watchman in Pieces: Surveillance, Literature, and Liberal Personhood* (New Haven: Yale University Press, 2013), 4.
23 Michel Foucault, *Discipline and Punish: The Birth of the Prison* (New York: Vintage Books, 1977), 216.
24 Regarding the "generalizable" nature of the panopticon, Foucault explains in a conversation with Jean-Pierre Barou and Michelle Perrot: "The Panopticon was at once a program and a utopia. But the theme of spatializing, observing, immobilizing, in a word disciplinary power was in fact already in Bentham's day being transcended by other and much more subtle mechanisms for the regulation of phenomena of population, controlling their fluctuations and compensating their irregularities. The tendency of Bentham's thought is archaic in the importance it gives to the gaze; but it is very modern in the general importance it assigns to techniques of

power" (Michel Foucault, *Power/Knowledge: Selected Interviews and Other Writings, 1972-1977* [New York: Pantheon Books, 1980], 146–65, here 159–60).

25 Regarding the asymmetric or, in Foucauldian parlance, "dissymmetric" power according to which the guardian in the central tower sees without being seen, Foucault remarks: "In his first version of the *Panopticon*, Bentham had also imagined an acoustic surveillance, operated by means of pipes leading from the cells to the central tower. In the *Postscript* he abandoned the idea, perhaps because he could not introduce into it the *principle of dissymmetry* and prevent the prisoners from hearing the inspector as well as the inspector hearing them" (Foucault, *Discipline and Punish*, 317n3, emphasis mine; see also 214).

26 Foucault, *Discipline and Punish*, 135.

27 "[T]he major effect of the Panopticon: to induce in the inmate a state of conscious and permanent visibility that assures the automatic functioning of power. So to arrange things that the surveillance is permanent in its effects, even if it is discontinuous in its action; that the perfection of power should tend to render its actual exercise unnecessary; that this architectural apparatus should be a machine for creating and sustaining a power relation independent of the person who exercises it; in short, that the inmates should be caught up in a power situation of which they are themselves the bearers" (Foucault, *Discipline and Punish*, 201).

28 Cf. Jean Baudrillard's eclectic meditation on the decline of panopticism and the emergence of simulacra in *Simulacra and Simulation* (Ann Arbor: University of Michigan Press, 1994), 1–42.

29 Gilles Deleuze, "Postscript on the Societies of Control," *October* 59 (1992): 3–7, here 3.

30 Deleuze, "Postscript on the Societies of Control," 3–4.

31 Deleuze, "Postscript on the Societies of Control," 5.

32 Deleuze, "Postscript on the Societies of Control," 4.

33 See Deleuze, "Postscript on the Societies of Control," 7, 4.

34 Paul Virilio, *The Vision Machine* (Bloomington: Indiana University Press, 1994), 59.

35 See Virilio, *The Vision Machine*, 62. "Aren't they also talking about the new technology of 'visionics': the possibility of achieving *sightless vision* whereby the video camera would be controlled by a computer? The computer would be responsible for the machine's—rather than the televiewer's—capacity to analyse the ambient environment and automatically interpret the meaning of events" (59).

36 Virilio, *The Vision Machine*, 65–66.

37 Virilio, *The Vision Machine*, 66, 70.

38 Jacques Lacan, *The Four Fundamental Concepts of Psychoanalysis* (New York: W. W. Norton, 1977), 84.

39 Lacan, *The Four Fundamental Concepts of Psychoanalysis*, 84.

40 See also Henry Krips, "The Politics of the Gaze: Foucault, Lacan and Žižek," *Culture Unbound: Journal of Current Cultural Research* 2 (2010): 91–102, here 94.

41 Jacques Lacan, "The Mirror Stage as Formative of the *I* Function as Revealed in Psychoanalytic Experience," in *Écrits: The First Complete Edition in English*, trans. Bruce Fink (New York: Norton, 2006), 75–81. On the changing implications of the concept of the "mirror stage" throughout Lacan's oeuvre, see Jay, *Downcast Eyes*, 339–71.

42 Slavoj Žižek, "Big Brother, or, the Triumph of the Gaze over the Eye," in *Ctrl Space: Rhetorics of Surveillance from Bentham to Big Brother*, ed. Levin, Frohne, and Weibel (Cambridge, MA: MIT Press, 2002), 224–27, here 225. Correspondingly, Žižek speaks of the "urgent need for the [...] Other's Gaze serving as the guarantee of the subject's being: 'I exist only insofar as I am looked at all the time'" (225).

43 Hans Blumenberg, *Shipwreck with Spectator: Paradigm of a Metaphor for Existence* (Cambridge, MA: MIT Press, 1997), 26.

44 Blumenberg, *Shipwreck with Spectator*, 54, 17.
45 Blumenberg, *Shipwreck with Spectator*, 54, 17, 39–40.
46 Blumenberg, *Shipwreck with Spectator*, 8, 35.
47 Niklas Luhmann, *Theory of Society* (Stanford: Stanford University Press, 2012), 1: 34.
48 Niklas Luhmann, *Art as a Social System* (Stanford: Stanford University Press, 2000), 60.
49 Luhmann, *Art as a Social System*, 63.
50 Luhmann, *Art as a Social System*, 63, 93.
51 *Oxford English Dictionary*, s.v. Similarly, *Merriam-Webster's Dictionary* defines surveillance as "the act of carefully watching someone or something, especially in order to prevent or detect a crime."

Works Cited

Baudrillard, Jean. *Simulacra and Simulation*. Ann Arbor, MI: University of Michigan Press, 1994.

Bentham, Jeremy. *The Panopticon Writings*. London: Verso, 1995.

Blumenberg, Hans. *Shipwreck with Spectator: Paradigm of a Metaphor for Existence*. Cambridge, MA: MIT Press, 1997.

Dandeker, Christopher. *Surveillance, Power and Modernity: Bureaucracy and Discipline from 1700 to the Present Day*. Cambridge: Polity Press, 1990.

Deleuze, Gilles. "Postscript on the Societies of Control." *October* 59 (1992): 3–7.

Foucault, Michel. *Discipline and Punish: The Birth of the Prison*. New York: Vintage Books, 1977.

Foucault, Michel. *Power/Knowledge: Selected Interviews and Other Writings, 1972–1977*. New York: Pantheon Books, 1980.

Heidegger, Martin. *Holzwege*. Frankfurt/M: Klostermann, 1977.

Heidegger, Martin. *The Question Concerning Technology and Other Essays*. Trans. William Lovitt. New York: Harper & Row, 1977.

Jay, Martin. *Downcast Eyes: The Denigration of Vision in Twentieth-Century French Thought*. Berkeley, CA: University of California Press, 1993.

Kammerer, Dietmar. *Bilder der Überwachung*. Frankfurt/M: Suhrkamp, 2008.

Krips, Henry. "The Politics of the Gaze: Foucault, Lacan and Žižek." *Culture Unbound: Journal of Current Cultural Research* 2 (2010): 91–102.

Lacan, Jacques. *The Four Fundamental Concepts of Psychoanalysis*. New York: W. W. Norton, 1977.

Lacan, Jacques. "The Mirror Stage as Formative of the *I* Function as Revealed in Psychoanalytic Experience." In *Écrits: The First Complete Edition in English*, trans. Bruce Fink, 75–81. New York: Norton, 2006.

Luhmann, Niklas. *Art as a Social System*. Stanford, CA: Stanford University Press, 2000.

Luhmann, Niklas. *Theory of Society*. Vol. 1. Stanford, CA: Stanford University Press, 2012.

Lyon, David. *The Electronic Eye: The Rise of Surveillance Society*. Cambridge: Polity, 1994.

Lyon, David. *Surveillance Studies: An Overview*. Cambridge: Polity Press, 2007.

Rosen, David, and Aaron Santesso. *The Watchman in Pieces: Surveillance, Literature, and Liberal Personhood*. New Haven, CT: Yale University Press, 2013.

Sartre, Jean-Paul. *Being and Nothingness: An Essay on Phenomenological Ontology*. London: Routledge, 2003.

Schmidt-Burkhardt, Astrit. “The All-Seer: God’s Eye as Proto-Surveillance.” In *Ctrl Space: Rhetorics of Surveillance from Bentham to Big Brother*, ed. Thomas Levin, Ursula Frohne, and Peter Weibel, 17–31. Cambridge, MA: MIT Press, 2002.

Schwering, Gregor. “Über das Auge triumphiert der Blick: Perspektiven des Voyerismus.” In *Big Brother: Beobachtungen*, ed. Friedrich Balke, Gregor Schwering, and Urs Stäheli, 129–50. Bielefeld: Transcript Verlag, 2000.

Seppänen, Janne. *The Power of the Gaze: An Introduction to Visual Literacy*. New York: Peter Lang International Academic Publishers, 2006.

Simmel, Georg. “Sociology of the Senses: Visual Interaction.” In *Introduction to the Science of Sociology*, ed. R. E. Park and W. W. Burgess, 356–61. Chicago, IL: University of Chicago Press, 1969.

Simmel, Georg. *Soziologie: Untersuchungen über die Formen der Vergesellschaftung*. Berlin: Duncker & Humblot, 1908.

Stolleis, Michael. *Das Auge des Gesetzes: Geschichte einer Metapher*. Munich: Verlag C. H. Beck, 2004.

Virilio, Paul. *The Vision Machine*. Bloomington: Indiana University Press, 1994.

Weber, Max. *Economy and Society: An Outline of Interpretive Sociology*. Berkeley, CA: University of California Press, 1978.

Weinstein, Deena, and Michael Weinstein. “On the Visual Constitution of Society: The Contributions of Georg Simmel and Jean-Paul Sartre to a Sociology of the Senses.” *History of European Ideas* 5.4 (1984): 349–62.

Žižek, Slavoj. “Big Brother, or, the Triumph of the Gaze over the Eye.” In *Ctrl Space: Rhetorics of Surveillance from Bentham to Big Brother*, ed. Thomas Levin, Ursula Frohne, and Peter Weibel, 224–27. Cambridge, MA: MIT Press, 2002.

1 *Counter-Music*

Farocki's Theory of a New Image Type

Harun Farocki's 2004 installation *Counter-Music* explores the issue of surveillance. It probes different kinds of surveillance and, in so doing, delineates historical trajectories, juxtaposing, for instance, state surveillance under Louis XIV in late-seventeenth-century France (through public streetlights) and more recent modes of observation via surveillance cameras (through closed-circuit television [CCTV] systems). The tacit epicenter of Farocki's installation is the novel form of surveillance in which cameras are linked with automatic-recognition systems that no longer rely on human beings as observers: Human beings have been replaced by software designed to surveil. This new kind of surveillance, in which images are recorded and then "viewed" by automatic "eyes"—that is, analyzed by algorithmic software—generates what Farocki calls "operational images" to be used within systemic surveillance operations.

Counter-Music seeks to understand the questions that such an automated form of surveillance raises with regard to the notion of "the human" and of human affect (to the extent that it relies on the paradoxical efficacy of blind sight). Rather than providing a philosophical argument, a conceptually sound narrative that is presented in images, Farocki (and here the aesthetic rendering of his installation comes into play) seeks to think *through* images. His process of thinking transpires through the surveillance images he employs, images that are, by their very nature, not meant to be watched; for the most part, nothing is happening that would be worth watching. Hence the ever-increasing application of automatic-recognition systems, which analyze the monotonous images algorithmically and thereby assist or replace the easily distracted human eye. While Farocki explicitly thematizes this displacement of the human in his installation, a different and decidedly human dimension emerges in the course of his particular arrangement of surveillance footage and our concomitant task of reading these images. Farocki creates a complex network of cross-references, of adumbrated analogies that are not rendered explicit, as well as unambiguous correspondences that are figuratively undercut. Just as the human ceases to matter in the practice of surveillance, Farocki's enactment of surveillance compels it to reemerge. *Counter-Music* relates antipodally to its

DOI: 10.4324/9781003229834-2

subject matter: It demands a reading of surveillance images that these images seem to have left behind long ago.

I

Surveillance was at the center of Farocki's work for some two decades. This interest permeated such different projects as *Images of the World and the Inscription of War* (1995), *Workers Leaving the Factory* (1995), *Prison Images* (2000), *I Thought I Was Seeing Convicts* (2000), *Eye/Machine I, II, III* (2001–3), *War at a Distance* (2003), and *Counter-Music* (2004). In these works, Farocki explores surveillance in the city, the prison, the workplace, and the supermarket, in military warfare and medical research—often in light of their intertwinement in one and the same project. The various manifestations of surveillance in early twenty-first-century urban spaces lie at the center of *Counter-Music*. This installation, perhaps more emphatically than any of his other works, elucidates the degree to which surveillance is not merely a technical phenomenon, a (mechanical) means toward an (economic, political, social) end. Rather, surveillance presents itself as a cultural paradigm of our time, as a social "symptom"[1] that—and this is the kernel of Farocki's interest—manifests a new type of image, one that has thus far remained "under-theorized" and hence emerges as a subject in need of theoretical scrutiny.[2]

Notably, video surveillance, as depicted in *Counter-Music*, is less an isolated practice than a thoroughly integrated network, a network suffusing the French city of Lille's infrastructure in every possible way. Given the ever more prevalent application of surveillance technology in urban spaces, video surveillance—in addition to the established networks of electricity, telecommunications, gas, and water—appears as a sort of "fifth utility."[3] In the text accompanying the installation, Farocki lays out his initial plan for *Counter-Music*:

> The activation of the city only through diagrams, representations, measurements.
>
> - Gas use
> - Traffic light configurations
> - Electricity grids
> - Mobile phone networks
> - Railway line representations
>
> Plus surveillance cameras in train stations, power stations, at crossings, on motorways, etc.[4]

Conspicuously, the network of surveillance technology emerges in *Counter-Music* not merely as *contiguous* but as *interlaced* with other infrastructures:

for example, the sewage system, as becomes apparent in a sequence in which subterranean video cameras move through drainage pipes in search of defects. The intertitle reads: "We follow the cameras moving through the city's sewers. The camera checks the welding of the pipes. The veins of the city."[5] The traffic system, too, is seen to be tightly monitored: Traffic density, congestion, and accidents are detected and displayed via computer simulation. "In rich countries the streets fill up in the morning [...] circulating instead of sitting about. Metabolism of the city-body [...]." Soon after, Farocki contrasts the rhizomatic structures of urban surveillance with those of human blood vessels, which, like the city's sewers, can be monitored from within and checked for abnormalities or blockages. Curiously, this medical register is eventually retranslated into the urban sphere: The logic of modern urban planning frequently presents itself as one that equates *security* (guaranteed through video surveillance) and *cleanliness* (guaranteed through the expulsion of criminals)[6]—a nexus pointed to in Lille and especially in "Euralille," the business district in the center of the city where most of *Counter-Music* is shot. "Many cities whose industry has faded are building a new centre," an intertitle states, describing how the decline of the textile industry in Lille triggered a decidedly unhygienic process of urban decay, which came to a halt only when a new, closely monitored city center was built, one that promised new prosperity.[7]

Euralille appears, in Farocki's installation, as a controlled society: "The city is as rationalized and regulated as a production process," Farocki writes. Correspondingly, "the images which today determine the day of the city are [...] control images":

> Representations of traffic regulation by car, train or metro, representations determining the height at which mobile phone network transmitters are fixed, and where the holes in the networks are. Images from thermo-cameras to discover heat loss from buildings. And digital models of the city, portrayed with fewer shapes of buildings or roofs than were used in the 19th century when planned industrial cities arose, amongst them the Lille agglomeration. Despite their boulevards, promenades, market places, arcades and churches, these cities are already machines for living and working.[8]

The "machine" Lille—with its subterranean monitoring of the sewage system, its tracking equipment for satellite television, its control systems of automobile, metro, and train transportation, as well as automated CCTV systems recording pedestrian traffic—in many ways appears to embody what (in Deleuzian parlance) has often been described as a "control society."[9] Yet exactly what characterizes a control society as exemplified by Farocki's Lille, and, more important, wherein lies Lille's relevance to Farocki's theoretical project?

II

Farocki's Lille is, as displayed on a computer-simulated map, above all, a major transportation hub: thirty-eight minutes to Brussels, one hour to Paris, two hours to London, three hours to Cologne, Amsterdam, and Luxembourg. What links Lille with these cities is the French high-speed-rail service, and so it appears consequential that Farocki moves his camera into "the high-speed train control centre in Lille (TGV)," where countless cameras send images to be displayed on numerous monitors. Cut to the "control centre for the Metro in Lille (Transpole)" and the commenting intertitle: "Images from 1,200 cameras arrive at this control centre." With a perpendicular panning shot along the control monitors, Farocki directs our attention unequivocally to the side of the "surveillance system" rather than to the "surveilled subject."[10]

The many surveillance monitors function here as an extension of the cameras' vigilant eyes and, as such, epitomize an ominous futuristic scenario (recalling Michael Klier's film *The Giant*)[11] of total surveillance. In spite of the futuristic appearance of this technology, a topos emerges that can be traced back to Greek mythology, famously embodied by the giant Argus Panoptes, who had eyes all over his body and could look in every direction, all day and all night (Figure 1.1).[12] Like a metamorphosis of Argus Panoptes, the metro control center in *Counter-Music* stands guard with a hundred eyes, some of which never sleep. Argus is ordered by Hera to watch the nymph Io, whom

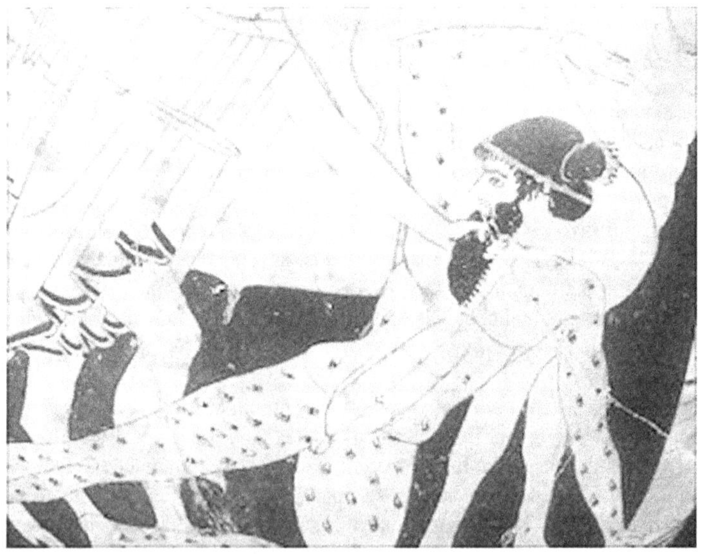

Figure 1.1 Hermes slaying Argus Panoptes, Athenian red-figure vase. Fifth century B.C., Kunsthistorisches Museum, Vienna.

Figure 1.2 Counter-Music (Harun Farocki, 2004).

Zeus had seduced; the personnel in Lille's metro control center are ordered to watch the life of the city, which is technologically mediated by the many simultaneously recording cameras and monitors displaying the transmitted images (Figure 1.2). These control *monitors*, of course, can never broadcast more than a fragmented image of the world, a fragmented "world picture," as one might say with Heidegger.[13] Etymologically they invoke a highly charged frame of reference. The classical Latin *monitor* is derived from the verb *monere* ("to advise, warn, remind") and carries, according to the *Oxford English Dictionary*, not only the contemporary meaning "to observe [...] esp. for the purpose of regulation or control" but also the more portentous connotation of giving a "warning as to conduct." The array of control monitors Farocki shows us invokes, then, not only the all-seeing Argus Panoptes but also a Christian concept of an omnipotent God, whose gaze is always a gaze from *above*, just as the surveillance cameras' gaze in *Counter-Music* is typically a gaze from above (as exemplified by footage of a group of adolescents sitting about in Euraville, or of passengers trying to board a subway). The understanding of the surveillance cameras' gaze as the secular equivalent of God's gaze is one that Farocki, in his film *Prison Images*, renders explicit: "The [surveillance] camera which the inmates go past has taken the place of God."[14]

Conspicuously, *Counter-Music* does not merely consider conventional electronic interface surveillance through video cameras but also surveillance

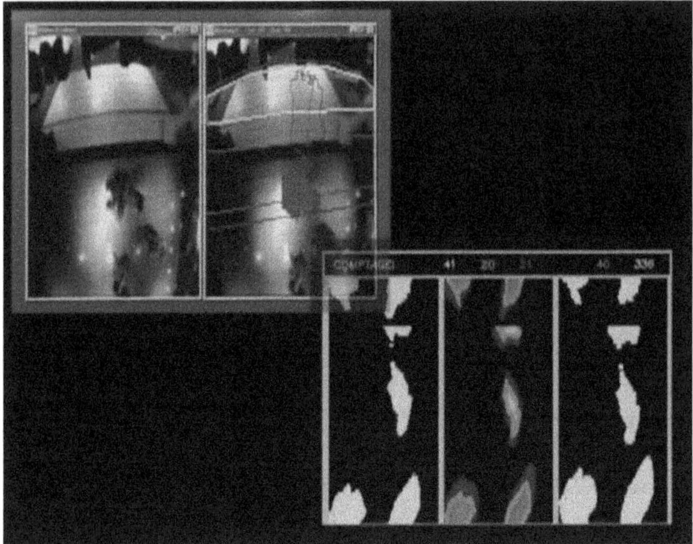

Figure 1.3 *Counter-Music* (Harun Farocki, 2004).

systems that are linked with pattern-recognition software. Such automated surveillance systems, exemplified by the repeatedly shown "intelligent" scene-monitoring that can identify "people who don't budge," evoke, in their tendency to reduce human beings to numbers and analyze them algorithmically, Deleuze's conception of the "control society." We see a monitor that displays surveillance footage of human beings passing through a train station (Figure 1.3); with it is the intertitle, "This software counts the people passing by/Whereby it is not easy to make out the individual in the mass." Farocki notes that both Ruttmann and Vertov, in their city films *Berlin: Symphony of a Great City* (1927) and *Man with a Movie Camera* (1929), respectively, "envisaged something different. For them, the crowd was not a lump to be dissected and rendered as numbers." What sort of conceptual shift are we dealing with, then, when human beings are conceived of as blocks to be encoded numerically? In his enigmatic "Postscript on the Societies of Control," Deleuze argues that the traditional panoptic model that Foucault found to characterize eighteenth- and nineteenth-century *disciplinary societies* has been more and more replaced by modern *control societies*, which are less centralized and less enclosed yet, surprisingly, no less tightly regulated and controlled.[15] Farocki, in a piece about *Prison Images*, writes about just that: "Deregulation does not by any means imply a reduction of control. [...] Deleuze outlined the vision of a society of controls which he said would replace disciplinary society."[16] No doubt it is this late Deleuzian text that inspired Farocki's characterization of surveillance technology as he finds it in Lille, including its tendency to view the urban crowd as a "lump to be dissected and rendered as numbers." "The disciplinary societies," Deleuze notes,

> have two poles: the signature that designates the *individual*, and the [...] administrative numeration that indicates his or her position within a *mass*. [...] In the societies of control, on the other hand, what is important is no longer [...] a signature [...] but a code [...]. We no longer find ourselves dealing with the mass/individual pair. Individuals have become "*dividuals*," and masses, samples, data.[17]

When "individuals" are reduced to "dividuals"—or, to list some of the formulations one encounters in the surveillance-studies literature, to "data doubles,"[18] "data shadows,"[19] "data images,"[20] or "databased selves"[21]—or, in Farocki's plain words, to "numbers," then it becomes clear not only how the *systems* of surveillance have developed but also how the *subjects* of surveillance have been exposed to a radical reconceptualization. Farocki's *Counter-Music* accomplishes nothing short of an investigation into the anthropological and media-theoretical consequences precipitated by new surveillance technologies. If earlier we asked what characterizes a control society such as Lille, and, more important, wherein Lille's relevance to Farocki's theoretical project can be found, then two provisional answers present themselves. First, on the anthropological level, we are dealing with a new conception of "the human" as data-conglomerate. Second, on a media-theoretical level, Farocki describes new kinds of images: automated surveillance images, which he dubs "operational images."

III

"The images which today determine the day of the city are operational images," Farocki claims.[22] As he explains, "Rather than these images being supposed to represent the production process, they are the production process."[23] Operational images certainly abound in *Counter-Music*, including numerous digital representations of traffic regulation. And of course, operational images can be found in other contexts as well. In *Images of the World and the Inscription of War*, for instance, we learn about the application of operational images to control robots in the automobile industry;[24] in Farocki's installation *I Thought I Was Seeing Convicts,* operational images track the movement of customers in a supermarket, and in *Eye/Machine* they promise the targeted impact of military projectiles, abetting the utopian conception of a "humane war." If one asks what exactly "operational images" are, Farocki explains that by the term he means "pictures, made neither to entertain nor to inform [...]. These are images that do not represent an object, but rather are part of an operation."[25] He goes on to explain that the term was inspired by Roland

Barthes's *Mythologies* (1957/64), specifically the afterword and the distinction Barthes draws there:

> I must return here to the distinction between the language of objects and meta-language. If I am a lumberjack and I name the tree that I am chopping down, I say—whatever the form of the sentence may be—*the tree*, and I do not speak *about* the tree. [...] If I am not a lumberjack, though, I cannot say *the tree*, I can only talk *of* and *about it*.[26]

Operational images do not talk *of* or *about* something; instead, they speak by way of what they do or generate or precipitate. It is not their constative assertions that are relevant but their performative thrust, their functional valence concerning a defined operation.

Against the backdrop of Vertov's and Ruttman's city films Farocki notes, "I too want to 'remake' the city films, *but with different images*." What renders the images incorporated in *Counter-Music* different (the surveillance images in general and those inflected by automatic-recognition systems, i.e., operational images, in particular) is, generally speaking, the absence of human beings, and that on at least three levels. First, in contrast to the seeming ubiquity of the cameraman in Vertov's *Man with a Movie Camera*, Farocki's *Counter-Music* assembles "Images *without* a cameraman/camerawoman," as one intertitle pronounces, thus gesturing at the absence of the human on the production side of surveillance images. Second, modern surveillance systems' tendency to reduce human beings to "numbers" invokes the nonexistence of human beings as the *subject matter* of surveillance. Finally, as one of the installation's last intertitles suggests, surveillance images such as the ones arriving in the control centers in the city of Lille are often "processed by a programme. Programmes reducing the amount of work for the viewer or abolishing it." In line with the disappearance of human beings as producers and subject matter of these newly configured images, humans also fall on the *recipient's* side of the equation.

Indeed, the increasing "abolition" of humans in modern-day surveillance is one that Farocki explicitly problematizes by way of analogy with the textile industry in Lille. Just as human beings, in the course of industrialization and the automation of weaving, have turned into "appendages of the apparatus," so the human eye, according to Farocki's suggestive montage, has been relegated, in line with the automation of surveillance via automatic-recognition systems, to "appendages of the apparatus" (Figures 1.4 and 1.5). The labor of weaving, as well as the labor of seeing, is ever less dependent on the involvement of human beings—an observation that led Paul Virilio to speak of the ever-increasing importance of "vision machines."[27] *Counter-Music* links the thematized history of weaving with the history of seeing; what constitutes the gist of Farocki's argument by analogy is the increasing displacement of human beings from technical operations,[28] the displacement of human beings as "operational" constituents in the weaving industry and, correspondingly the surveillance industry.

Figure 1.4 *Counter-Music* (Harun Farocki, 2004).

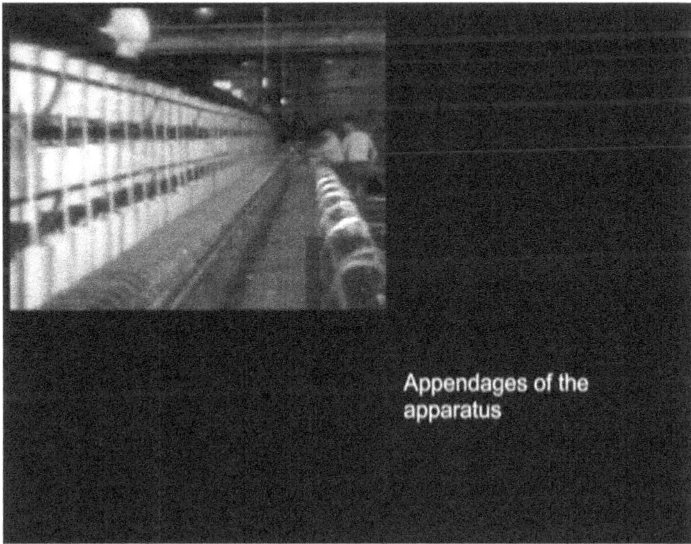

Figure 1.5 *Counter-Music* (Harun Farocki, 2004).

IV

Yet how does the gradual abolition of human beings relate to the poetic fabric of Farocki's installation, in particular his intricate split-screen aesthetic that emphatically engages the viewer? How can we understand the paradoxical combination of the underwhelming and undramatic nature of "found footage" surveillance images and Farocki's stratified ways of arranging that very footage? What is the promise of this aesthetic that neither edifies nor entertains but instead imposes considerable strain on our ability and our willingness to contemplate?[29] Just as Farocki, with respect to "operational images," speaks of the abolition of work to be accomplished by human beings, so do we as viewers of Farocki's installation perceive the tenacious demand—triggered by his complex split-screen aesthetic—to engage and make sense of it. Let us consider an example: We see the unique L-shaped office building, the Tour de Lille (designed by Christian de Portzamparc), atop the Lille Europe railway station on the left track of Farocki's installation; simultaneously, on the right track, a piece of trash blows across the pavement, a bit of discarded paper wrapping from a fast-food restaurant, it seems—we cannot quite make it out, and it does, after all, not really seem to matter. But what does it mean that something does or does not matter, and how do we deem one image meaningful and another not? Farocki, to be sure, does not provide unequivocal answers to these questions. For a solid fifty-five seconds, the camera follows this piece of trash as it dances across the pavement, jostled by the wind (Figure 1.6).

Figure 1.6 Counter-Music (Harun Farocki, 2004)

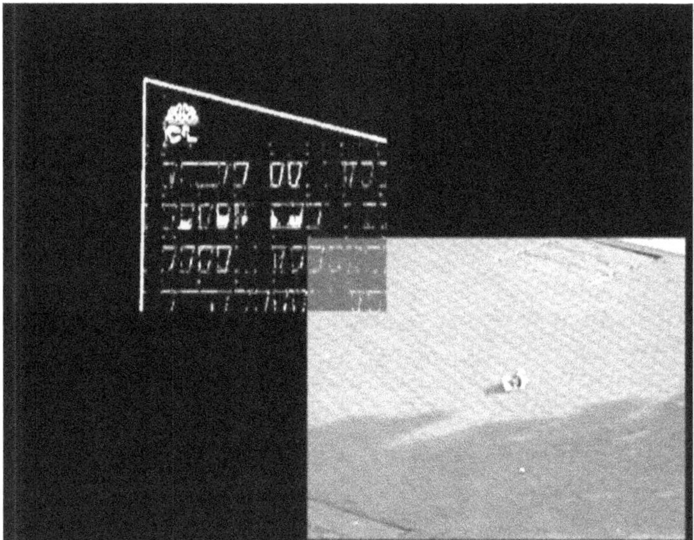

Figure 1.7 Counter-Music (Harun Farocki, 2004).

As if the questions of meaning and intention and the possibility of meaning without author and without intention had not been raised emphatically enough, the camera makes us watch yet another piece of trash, again on the right track and parallel to the L-shaped office building in Euralille on the left track. This time a discarded plastic bag is carried across the cobblestones. As we ponder the possible meanings of this enigmatic sequence, the L-shaped office building, depicted in the left image track, transitions from conventional surveillance-camera imagery to a series of surveillance-camera images analyzed by algorithmic-recognition software, "operational images" that invoke the gradual displacement of human beings as viewers, in that they do not require a contemplative reading but assume a calculated interface position within a defined operation (Figures 1.7–1.9).

The paradox here results from the peculiar juxtaposition of the two image tracks, the "soft montage," as Farocki would say. The surveillance footage showing the wrapping paper and the plastic bag in the right image track raises questions regarding the humanly conceivable meaning of such images. Functioning exactly as antipode, the operational images in the left image track insist on the dispensability of human viewers by allocating the task of "viewing" to machines. The succession of images as well as the tension between the two tracks could undoubtedly be read in different ways as well, and it is precisely the ambiguity emanating from the two-screen installation that prompts its performative thrust. Our semantic involvement in the installation, our

Figure 1.8 Counter-Music (Harun Farocki, 2004).

Figure 1.9 Counter-Music (Harun Farocki, 2004).

"reading," manifests the very opposite of what *Counter-Music* seems to be all about, namely, the abolition of the human worker in modern control society. Whereas the conceptual center of what Farocki describes in his installation is the operational image, which excludes human beings, the installation derives its performative traction from his two-screen "soft montage," which does require human beings. Farocki, as it were, (performatively) undoes the very dynamic he describes (constatively), and it is this peculiar interplay between content and form or matter and manner that emerges again and again. Again and again, the center of Farocki's theoretical argumentation, the *operational image*, is figuratively thwarted by the rhetorical efficacy of the *soft montage*.

In an article delineating his aesthetics of "soft montage," Farocki portrays this split-screen approach as follows: "There is succession as well as simultaneity in a double projection, the relationship of an image to the one that follows as well as the one beside it; a relationship to the preceding as well as to the concurrent one." Farocki draws on a metaphor to elucidate: "Imagine three double bonds jumping back and forth between the six carbon atoms of a benzene ring; I envisage the same ambiguity in the relationship of an element in an image track to the one succeeding or accompanying it."[30] Farocki draws on this method of double projection for the first time in *Interface* (1995), a work commissioned by a museum in Villeneuve D'Ascq near Lille in the mid-1990s. "For the first time, I had the chance to work with two images, something familiar to me from the 1970s avant-garde," he explains.[31] His second double projection was the 2000 *I Thought I Was Seeing Convicts*, where we encounter a technique that will return in *Counter-Music*—namely, the tendency

> to use one track as the main text and the other track as its commentary or its footnotes. The second track lent itself to working with anticipation and reprise, with trailer and cliff-hanger. It is a seductive way of easily achieving an effect, comparable to the shot/reverse shot in a single-strip film. [...] It was possible to cut in a title on one track whilst the image continued on the other, so that the viewer had the choice—amongst other things, of relating the title to one track or to both. It also lent itself to interrupting the image flow on both tracks with a title, as well as showing the same image on both tracks. It seemed to me that although it is possible to do with one image everything one can do with two, it would be still easier to create a soft montage with two tracks. More trial, less assertion. Equivocality can be attained with the simplest means.[32]

The transposition of the shot-reverse-shot technique into a single film strip,[33] this two-track technique of soft montage, allowing for "more trial" and "less assertion," subsequently appears in *Eye/Machine* (2001–3), then in *Counter-Music* (2004) and a number of other installations, including *Comparison via a Third* (2007); *Deep Play* (2007), where no fewer than twelve image tracks are put into dialogue; and finally in *Serious Games* (2009/2010) and *The Silver and the Cross* (2010). In all these works, the typical temporal sequence of images is spatially expanded to create an effect of a "simultaneity," an "And rather than Or."[34] Regarding his style in general and his technique of "soft montage" in particular, Farocki elaborates: "One image doesn't take the place of the previous one, but supplements it, re-evaluates it, balances it."[35] This mode of supplementation, reevaluation, and balancing describes individual sequences as well as the overall economy of the installation, including its tendency to repeat sequences and suspend and, more often than not, continue individual narrative strands, allowing for a multifarious space that provokes a host of associative links and emphatically corroborates our role as human (rather than machinic),[36] creative spectators.[37]

Given this background, it might serve our understanding of Farocki's style to scrutinize yet another example from *Counter-Music*. Recall the aforementioned footage of workers in a weaving factory and the intertitle "Appendages of the apparatus." Cut (in the left track) to footage of textile workers leaving the factory and (in the right track) to the obliquely commenting intertitle "Today, almost every city has memories of an industrial past." The right track now picks up the footage of workers leaving the factory and shows these images as they are processed by an automatic-recognition system (Figures 1.10 and 1.11).

Figure 1.10 *Counter-Music* (Harun Farocki, 2004).

Figure 1.11 Counter-Music (Harun Farocki, 2004).

The paradoxes alluded to above are here solidified: First, Farocki reminds us of the gradual displacement of humans from the production process in the course of industrialization; then he incorporates documentary footage showing workers leaving the factory (in the left image track); finally, he shows images of the exact same workers, yet in the format of operational images (in the right image track)—evoking our own exclusion as workers or, more precisely, as viewers of images that are not intended to be seen by humans.[38] Just as the factory workers could not keep up with the demands of modern times, so we, it seems, have largely become superfluous in the face of operational images. Farocki confronts us with our ineptness vis-à-vis this new image species, yet he does so in a most meandering way, always immersed in the image at issue, suspending any theoretical generalization, often at the expense of narrative strands that do not fit in and poetic insinuations that do not add up. Ironically, it is precisely this authority in matters of meaning and interpretation transferred to us that performs—as far as our involvement as introspective thinkers is concerned—the opposite of what Farocki appears to observe throughout, namely, the abolition of human beings as factory workers and, correspondingly, as image workers.

V

The displacement of the human as *viewer*, in addition to his role as *producer* and *subject matter* (in the case of operational images engendered by automatic-image-recognition software), is ultimately what distinguishes the epistemology of modern-day surveillance from that of the cinema, as exemplified by Vertov's and Ruttmann's films. Farocki's installation offers, among other things, a theoretical comparison of surveillance images and cinematic images, and perhaps this is the moment to address the peculiar status of those two other filmmakers in *Counter-Music*. Needless to say, Vertov's and Ruttmann's films serve, on a basic level, as a model as far as the tradition of city films is concerned. Farocki writes:

> When I was asked to make a contribution to the exhibition [*La ville qui fait signes*], I instantly recalled the city films by Ruttmann and Vertov. Both succeeded in reading the city and in making it readable. They picked up on everyday happenings, hardly showing anything but that which everyone has seen before. They did not narrate a special day but one like any other. And yet their films were exciting. By discovering and revealing the lines of force in the undefined events, they dramatised the present.[39]

Yet Farocki is keenly aware of the dangers of transposing Vertov's and Ruttmann's early twentieth-century approach onto an early twenty-first-century project:

> When a few years ago in Berlin, Thomas Schadt set about making a remake of *Berlin—die Symphonie der Großstadt*, he attempted a reconstruction by seeking sequences in today's city similar to each of those used by Ruttmann. Whilst one can show images today of people streaming to work from their means of transport, it becomes all too obvious that there are hardly any large industries left in today's cities. And that the machine rhythm no longer makes a melody. Mass society is no longer spectacular. Spread-out hours of work, the non-representability of most working processes [*die Unanschaulichkeit der meisten Arbeitsabläufe*], reduced density of residence, all go to rob Ruttmann's imitators of strength.[40]

The evanescence of the industrial sector and the rise of the service industry correspond, according to Farocki, to a certain shift in vision: While Vertov's and Ruttmann's images were appropriate to reveal "the lines of force" of early twentieth-century metropolitan life and "dramatize" their present, the early twenty-first-century urban life Farocki finds himself confronted with in Lille is no longer "spectacular" and indeed has become "unrepresentable" or "undepictable" (*unanschaulich*).

It is precisely this "unspectacular" and "undepictable" quality of early twenty-first-century urban life that presents the key challenge for Farocki's project. Of course, Farocki seeks to develop and update the tradition of the city film. Yet given the technological developments, especially in the surveillance sector, this requires some sort of break with his predecessors. The installation's title, *Counter-Music*, testifies to this break, or rather to Farocki's repudiation of the means as they still came to bear in Ruttmann's and Vertov's films. In contrast to (or by *countering*) these "symphonic"[41] city films of the early twentieth century, Farocki's city film assembles—beyond all dramatization, and beyond all spectacle—images that "are produced today as an administrative measure,"[42] operational images of the regulation of car, train, metro, and other traffic. In contradistinction to Vertov's and Ruttmann's cinematic images, these operational images are generated not to be viewed by human beings, with the possible objective of contemplation or aesthetic gratification, but for the purpose of a specifically defined technical operation.

Counter-Music provides a number of examples where cinematic images and surveillance images are directly juxtaposed, and it may be rewarding to probe one of those instances in some detail. Roughly five minutes into the installation, Farocki invokes Ruttmann's famous city film with the following intertitle: "Walter Ruttmann begins with a train ride. 'Berlin—Symphony of a Great City' Germany 1927." We are presented with excerpts from Ruttmann's film, rapidly cut images of spinning train wheels, of rails and switch plates, and, time and again—through the windows of the racing train—images of treetops and telephone poles, moving images that enact or invoke, as in a mise en abyme, the experience of the cinematic gaze (Figure 1.12). These

Figure 1.12 *Counter-Music* (Harun Farocki, 2004).

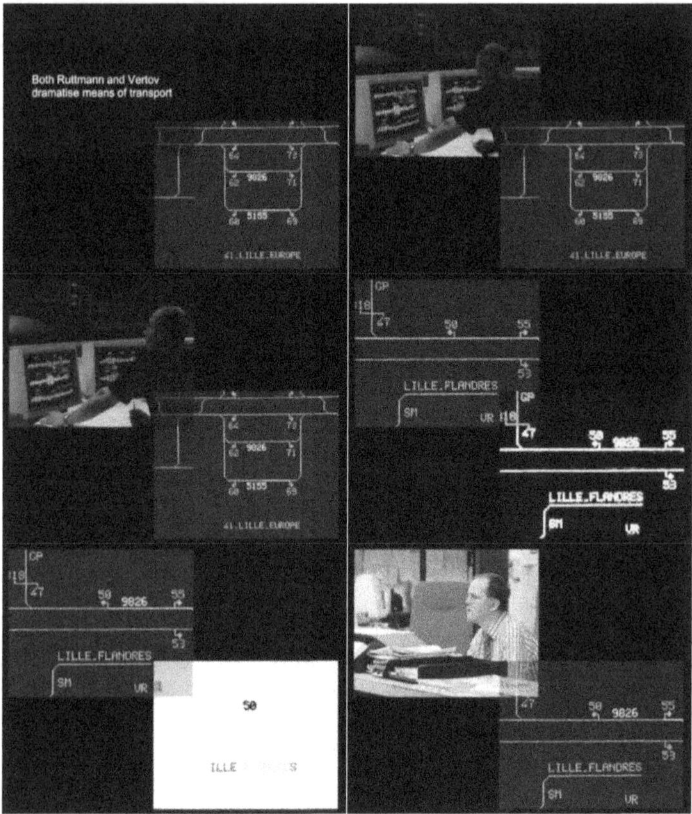

Figure 1.13 *Counter-Music* (Harun Farocki, 2004).

cinematic images, which can hardly be surpassed in their dramatic velocity (owing partly to the propulsive soundtrack Farocki adds to Ruttmann's film), are now contrasted with the contemporary images of the high-speed train passing through Lille. Significantly, twenty-first-century images present themselves as diagrammatic surveillance images, whose monotony and lack of plasticity in no way compare to the high-speed ride of the TGV but instead visualize the corresponding administrative processes (Figure 1.13). Cut then to Vertov's *Man with a Movie Camera*, specifically the breathtaking scene depicting "the man with a movie camera" in the act of capturing a rapidly approaching train via a low-angle point-of-view shot (Figure 1.14). If we compare the medium-specificity of cinematic images with that of surveillance images, the emphasis on the composition—the creative authorship so critical to cinematic images—is clearly absent from surveillance footage.

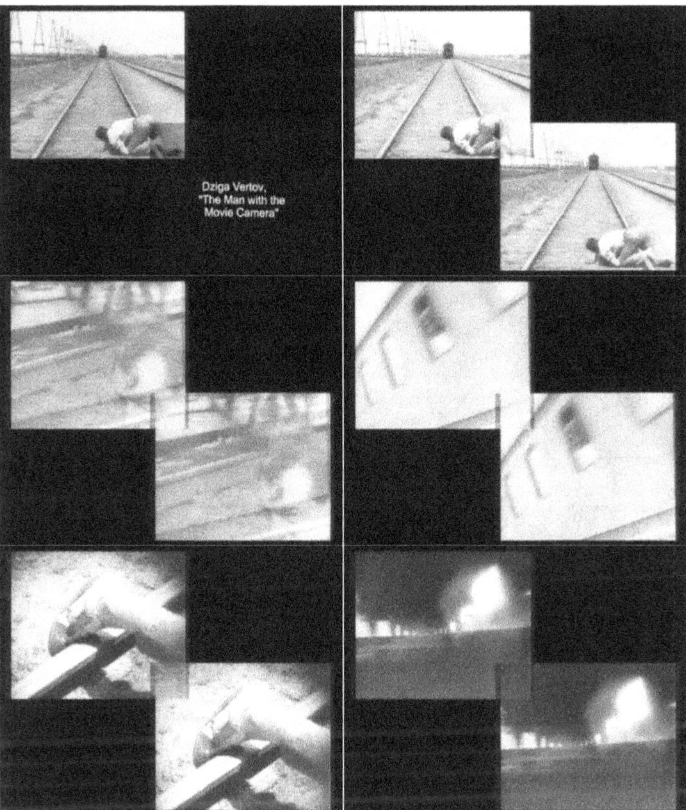

Figure 1.14 *Counter-Music* (Harun Farocki, 2004).

This difference, unsurprisingly, translates into the affective temperature of the respective media. "Both Ruttmann and Vertov dramatise means of transport," an intertitle states, hinting at the "extremely undramatic" quality of the surveillance images, with their comparative lack of "the most common means of condensation" such as "camera movements or edits."[43] At this point, yet another differentiating mark between the aesthetics of cinema and the aesthetics of surveillance imagery is evoked, namely, the expectation that cinematic images will be *seen* by some spectator (whose implied spectatorship may or may not have informed the production of the cinematic artwork from the outset). Most surveillance images, by contrast, are not intended to be viewed by anybody and—unless an exceptional occurrence like a robbery or riot requires their review—are indeed never seen by anyone but simply deleted or discarded.[44]

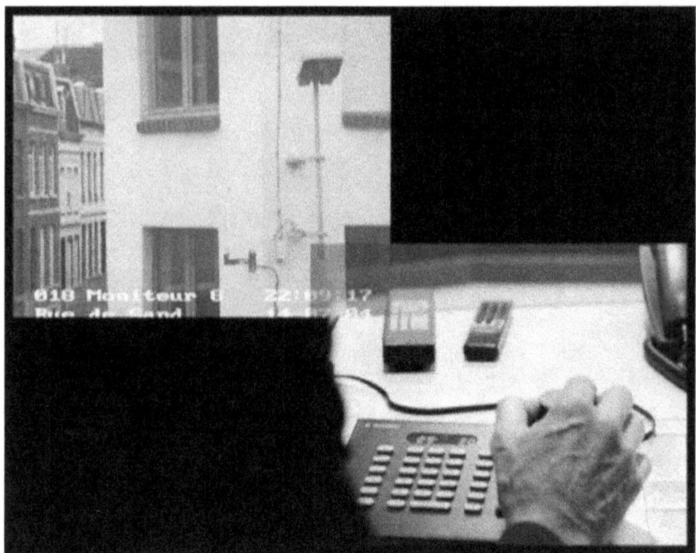

Figure 1.15 Counter-Music (Harun Farocki, 2004).

VI

The ever more pressing questions that need asking then are these: Wherein lies the unique quality of this relatively new species of surveillance image? What attributes does Farocki's installation evoke with regard to this new medium, a medium that he rightly characterizes as "under-theorized"?[45] A comparatively unequivocal response to these questions emerges with a sequence in *Counter-Music* that Farocki shoots "on 14 July 04 (national holiday)." In the right half of the installation's split screen, we follow security personnel handling the joystick of a surveillance control panel; in the left image track, we see a street lamp (Figure 1.15). With this the commentary: "We directed the surveillance cameras towards streetlights to catch the moment when they light up. We are not hunting in the wild—we are shooting animals which have already been captured." What do we make of this hunting metaphor? On the one hand, the metaphor appears to suggest that since we know that the street lamps will light up at some point, since we are waiting for the actualization of an "event" that we can already anticipate, this "moment when they light up" is comparable to an animal that has already been captured. In line with the temporality of surveillance imagery—the future perfect[46]—one could say: "The streetlights will have lit up." However, the situation described here does *not* describe the typical event structure of surveillance—hence the not quite authentic ("We are not hunting in the wild") quality of this "hunt" whose outcome is already

Figure 1.16 *Counter-Music* (Harun Farocki, 2004).

predetermined ("We are shooting animals which have already been captured"). For what characterizes surveillance is precisely not the waiting for a particular event, is precisely not the tension, the anticipation of, say, a happy end, so familiar from the movies. Surveillance images are devoid of dramatic suspense, as is illustrated by Farocki's juxtaposition to Vertov's film. His juxtaposition of the bored gaze of a human monitor and a rapid car ride from Vertov's *Man with a Movie Camera* underscores this quality of surveillance imagery (Figure 1.16).

Instead of dramatic development, surveillance is empty time, ongoingness, and monotony, until the next surely occurring yet not quite definable event.[47] This empty time structure, in turn, determines the expectation of the viewer of surveillance images, articulated in *Counter-Music* by the words "We whiled away the time spent waiting." The whiling away, the sameness, that sense of boredom, describes the typical reception of surveillance images, a reception that may well be aligned with a certain hope for the arrival of an event but must acknowledge uneventfulness as a distinguishing quality of surveillance.[48] The surveillance cameras in Lille through which Farocki allows us to look implicate us—even if under artificial conditions ("We are not hunting in the wild")—in the experience of this ambivalent gaze. This is a gaze that might anticipate the eventual actualization of an event, the lighting up of the streetlights, yet it is bound to endure the monotony, the lack of any action, for most of the time, and is, in the course of waiting, presented no "dramatic

Figure 1.17 Counter-Music (Harun Farocki, 2004).

spectacle" other than the close-up of a discarded plastic bag, caught in a tree and caressed by the wind (Figure 1.17).

At this point in the installation, another intertitle raises the question "Are these images deliberate or chance?" In contrast to the cinematic images by Vertov and Ruttmann, it seems to be precisely the lack of authoriality, deliberation, and human intention that presents itself as distinctively characteristic of surveillance images.[49] The camera's eye merely records; it is a cold eye, as Farocki says,[50] an eye that does not want to see and seems unfettered by all affect. Yet what does it mean that an image does (or does not) have meaning, that it is inflected by some sort of intention? What does it mean if a viewer can (or cannot) find edification in an aesthetic composition, the skillful dramatization of events, punctuated by *kairos*, the right moment,[51] and by *telos*, an ultimate aim? These are questions that surveillance images confront us with and that constitute their theoretically underexplored, novel quality. Farocki compares, in a 1983 review of Michael Klier's film *The Giant*, the novelty of these images with the feeling of novelty shared by the beholders of the very first photographs. "The electronic cameras you can now find everywhere (usually angled downwards from above) for observation and surveillance," he remarks,

> produce images day and night, year in, year out. [...] Seeing these shots in sequence creates a kind of pensive reflection similar to the doubts following

> the appearance of photography. Early photography showed, which can always be the case again, that you can have other kinds of pictures than just those of important people, objects and events. Random images, since they are as much pictures as those taken deliberately, raise the question of what status, significance, meaning—and intention—are supposed to be.[52]

These lines, written roughly two decades before *Counter-Music*, anticipate, in condensed form, the crucial questions regarding surveillance images that would be more rigorously explored in the 2004 installation. They prefigure the eventless temporality and profoundly undramatic feel of most surveillance images as well as the nonexistence of an author, that is, the lack of any *intention* behind the images. Farocki elaborates on his interest in the idiosyncratic nature of surveillance images, which, in contrast to cinematic images, are

> not cropped and framed in order to compress space and time. [...] Images that appear so inconsequential that they are not stored—the tapes are erased and are used again. Generally the images are stored and archived only in exceptional cases, but exceptional cases one is sure to encounter. Such images challenge the artist who is interested in a meaning that is *not authorial and intentional*, an artist interested in a sort of beauty that is not calculated.[53]

Surveillance images are images that are neither cropped nor framed, devoid of *kairos* and *telos*, made to be deleted, by no author, with no intention. These, then, are, in Farocki's vein, the parameters of a theory of surveillance imagery.

Coda

Farocki's invocation of surveillance images' "uncalculated beauty" is, of course, in some respects paradoxical, given that the category of beauty, implicitly or explicitly, presupposes a beholder who can apprehend beauty as such. Yet surveillance images are for the most part not viewed by anyone, since most of what they record indeed is inconsequential, devoid of anything that might be of potential interest. For the type of surveillance images that Farocki dubs "operational images," namely, surveillance images analyzed by automatic-recognition systems, this holds true all the more given that such systems are designed to spare the human viewer the drudgery of viewing the infinite quantity of surveillance images. This is precisely the point where an abyss opens that pervades Farocki's installation from the first minute to the last. On the one hand, Farocki shows us images whose "meaning [...] is *not* [...] *intentional*." At the same time, we, Farocki's audience, are unmistakably implicated as far as our reflective capacity is concerned, our ability to disentangle the associative links that his "soft montage" precipitates. While Farocki's operational images allude to the abolition of human observers, his aesthetic emphatically demands our involvement and, as such, challenges and disturbs what *Counter-Music* seems to be about. Farocki has said with regard to surveillance images that "their continuous message is that what they show is not important."[54] One is tempted to turn this claim against his "found footage" installation and argue that *Counter-Music*'s "continuous message is that what [it shows] is not important." That we nonetheless invest ourselves in a reading of *Counter-Music* and find it, in perhaps not quite discernible ways, important might, after all, be attributable to its intended beauty.

Notes

1 David Lyon, *Surveillance Studies: An Overview* (Cambridge: Polity, 2007), 161; Dietmar Kammerer, *Bilder der Überwachung* (Frankfurt/M: Suhrkamp, 2008), 268.

2 Harun Farocki, *Bilderschatz* (Cologne: Buchhandlung Walther König, 1999), 8; Harun Farocki and Wolfgang Ernst, "Towards an Archive for Visual Concepts," in *Working on the Sight-Lines*, ed. Thomas Elsaesser (Amsterdam: Amsterdam University Press, 2004), 261–86, here 275.

3 Stephen Graham, "Towards the Fifth Utility? On the Extension and Normalization of Public CCTV," in *Surveillance, Closed Circuit Television, and Social Control*, ed. Clive Norris, Jade Moran, and Gary Armstrong (Brookfield: Ashgate, 1989), 89–112, here 108.

4 Harun Farocki, "Contre-chant," in *La ville qui fait signes*, ed. Alain Guiheux (Paris: Éditions du Moniteur, 2004), 106–17, here 108.

5 *Counter-Music*, directed by Harun Farocki (2004; Chicago: Video Data Bank, 2004), DVD. Unless otherwise noted, all italics in intertitles are mine.

6 Kammerer, *Bilder der Überwachung*, 63.

7 Farocki's sophisticated practice of appropriating existing images, his *détournement*, if you will, of course draws much of its force from montage. The imagistic juxtaposition of referential systems as different as urban canals, traffic, and the human body is driven by Farocki's penchant for developing his arguments in visual terms, in line with the "grammar of filmic motifs," as he put it in his Flusser lecture of 1999 (Farocki, *Bilderschatz*, 20; Farocki and Ernst, "Towards an Archive for Visual Concepts," 280). Farocki does not treat images on the basis of preconceived thematic categorizations but in terms of their visual idiosyncrasies. Interestingly, this understanding led Farocki, together with media theorists Friedrich Kittler and Wolfgang Ernst, to design a visual encyclopedia analogous to the renowned *Archive für Begriffsgeschichte* (literally, the "Archive for the History of Concepts"), published by the Academy of Sciences and Literature in Mainz. "This collection," Farocki holds, "has the advantage of not being bound to any lexical or systematic principle," and, as such, epitomizes the blueprint for the thus far unmaterialized project of an "archive of filmic expressions" (Farocki, *Bilderschatz*, 5; Farocki and Ernst, "Towards an Archive for Visual Concepts," 273; see also 265).

8 Farocki, "Contre-chant," 107.

9 Farocki himself emphasizes this correspondence to Deleuze in his essay "Controlling Observation," in *Harun Farocki: Imprint; Writings*, ed. Susanne Gaensheimer and Nicolaus Schafhausen (New York: Lukas and Sternberg, 2001), 306–21.

10 For a discussion of the "interactions between [...] the 'surveillance system' and the 'surveilled subject,'" see Lyon, *Surveillance Studies*, 75.

11 "I begrudged Michael Klier his idea of making a film entirely out of surveillance imagery (*Der Riese/The Giant*, 1983)," Farocki writes in his autobiographical collage, *Red Berta Goes Wandering without Love* (*Rote Berta geht ohne Liebe wandern* [Cologne: Strzelecki Books, 2009], 16; Farocki, "Written Trailers," in *Harun Farocki: Against What? Against Whom?*, ed. Antje Ehmann and Kodwo Eshun [London: Koenig Books, 2009], 220-41, here 227). Klier's *The Giant* is an experimental documentary film unprecedented insofar as it consists almost exclusively of surveillance footage—from an airport, railway station, department store, supermarket, streets, and so forth, thereby evoking the sense of a gigantic force overseeing the city.

12 In the fragment of a lost poem by Hesiod, Argus Panoptes is characterized as "great and strong Argus, who [...] looks every way [...]: sleep never fell upon his eyes; but he kept sure watch always" (Hesiod, *The Homeric Hymns and Homerica*, trans. Hugh G. Evelyn-White [Cambridge, MA: Harvard University Press, 1977], 273).

13 Martin Heidegger, "The Age of the World Picture," in *The Question Concerning Technology and Other Essays*, trans. William Lovitt (New York: Harper and Row, 1982), 129–30. See also Thomas Keenan, "Light Weapons," *Documents* 1–2 (1992): 147–58, here 147.

14 *Prison Images*, directed by Harun Farocki (2000; Berlin: Harun Farocki Filmproduktion, 2008), DVD.

15 Gilles Deleuze, "Postscript on the Societies of Control," *October* 59 (1992): 3–7. In a different context, Slavoj Žižek observes a "reversal of the Bentham-Orwellian notion of the Panopticon-society in which we are (potentially) 'observed always' and have no place to hide from the omnipresent gaze of the Power: today, anxiety seems to arise from the prospect of NOT being exposed to the Other's gaze all the time, so that the subject needs the camera's gaze as a kind of ontological guarantee of his/her being" (Žižek, "Big Brother, or, the Triumph of the Gaze over the Eye," in *Ctrl Space: Rhetorics of Surveillance from Bentham to Big Brother*, ed. Thomas Levin, Ursula Frohne, and Peter Weibel [Cambridge, MA: MIT Press, 2002], 224–27, here 225).

16 Farocki, "Controlling Observation," 318.

17 Deleuze, "Postscript on the Societies of Control," 5.

18 Kevin Haggerty and Richard Ericson, "The Surveillant Assemblage," *British Journal of Sociology* 41.4 (2000): 605–22; see also Lyon, *Surveillance Studies*, 87–88.

19 Alan F. Westin, *Privacy and Freedom* (New York: Atheneum, 1967).

20 David Lyon, *The Electronic Eye: The Rise of Surveillance Society* (Cambridge: Polity, 1994), 84, 206, 207.

21 Bart Simon, "The Return of Panopticism: Supervision, Subjection, and the New Surveillance," *Surveillance and Society* 3 (2005): 1–20.

22 Farocki, "Contre-chant," 107, translation modified; Harun Farocki, "Tagebuch: La ville qui fait signes," in *Weiche Montagen/Soft Montages*, ed. Yilmaz Dziewior (Cologne: Kunsthaus Bregenz, 2011), 104–8, here 105.

23 *War at a Distance*, directed by Harun Farocki (2003; Chicago: Video Data Bank, 2004), DVD.

24 On this film in particular, see the perceptive analysis by Nora Alter, "The Political Im/perceptible in the Essay Film: Farocki's *Images of the World and the Inscription of War*," *New German Critique* 68 (1996): 165–92.

25 Harun Farocki, "Phantom Images," *Public* 29 (2004): 12–24, here 17.

26 Roland Barthes, *Mythologies* (Paris: Seuil, 1957), 254; quoted in Farocki, "Phantom Images," 17.

27 Paul Virilio, *The Vision Machine* (Bloomington: Indiana University Press, 1994), especially 59–77.

28 The expulsion of human beings from sensorially charged work processes is also negotiated in Farocki's film *As You See*, where arithmetic (*Rechnen*) serves as a metaphor for the jettisoning of human beings from the craft of observing and,

similarly, from manual crafts such as weaving. On the "gradual replacement of sensuous images by what Farocki calls 'Rechnen,'" see Michael Cowan, "Rethinking the City Symphony after the Age of Industry: Harun Farocki and the 'City Film,'" *Intermédialités: Histoire et théorie des arts, des lettres et des techniques* 11 (2008): 69–86, here 71. The displacement of sensorially inflected human labor through technology is, differently configured, also addressed in the installation *I Thought I Was Seeing Convicts*, where the narrator states: "Whoever controls the technical means is considered powerful. The body alone does not count for much. Searches of cells [are] carried out by hand and with the aid of an electronic sensing device. This apparatus can detect even the smallest trace of a drug" (*I Thought I Was Seeing Convicts*, directed by Harun Farocki [2000; Chicago: Video Data Bank, 2000], DVD).

29 In his installation *Eye/Machine* Farocki characterizes operational images in terms of the lack of a "contemplative" viewer response and "edifying" effects; in "Phantom Images," the essay accompanying the installation, Farocki describes operational images with regard to the absence of "entertaining" qualities and "educational" intentions (Farocki, "Phantom Images," 17; *Eye/Machine*, directed by Harun Farocki [2001–3; Chicago: Video Data Bank, 2001–3], DVD).

30 Harun Farocki, "Cross Influence/Soft Montage," in *Against What? Against Whom?*, ed. Ehmann and Eshun, 69–74, here 70. Farocki first develops these thoughts together with film theorist Kaja Silverman in their jointly published work *Speaking about Godard* (New York: New York University Press, 1998), 142. See further the differently inflected metaphorization of the benzol molecule in Farocki's early film *Between Two Wars*. For a succinct commentary, see Volker Pantenburg, *Film als Theorie: Bildforschung bei Harun Farocki und Jean-Luc Godard* (Bielefeld: Transcript, 2006), 174.

31 Harun Farocki and Yilmaz Dziewior, "Gespräch, 23. Oktober 2010, Kunsthaus Bregenz," in *Weiche Montagen*, ed. Dziewior, 204–26, here 208.

32 Farocki, "Cross Influence/Soft Montage," 72–73.

33 "*Counter-Music* [...] with its original title *Contre-Chant*, which sounds like 'Contrechamp' (Engl. countershot), certainly [...] makes reference to film-immanent aspects, which are also emphasized by the split-screen format of the installation," Yilmaz Dziewior writes. "Harun Farocki's characteristic form of double projection is what enables him to produce both a regular succession of individual images and a simultaneity in their interrelationship. Despite the sometimes hard and unpredictable cuts, the jumping back and forth of images creates [...] soft montages" (Yilmaz Dziewior, "Harun Farocki: Weiche Montagen," in *Weiche Montagen*, ed. Dziewior, 10–14, here 12). Other critics who have commented on the "homophony" between the installation's original French title and the French "contrechamp" ("countershot" or "reverse shot") include Volker Pantenburg, "*Gegen-Musik*," in *Weiche Montagen*, ed. Dziewior, 98–103, here 98; and Christa Blüminger, "Memory and Montage: On the Installation *Counter-Music*," in *Against What? Against Whom?*, ed. Ehmann and Eshun, 101–9, here 102.

34 Farocki and Dziewior, "Gespräch," 206.

35 Harun Farocki and Rembert Hüser, "Nine Minutes in the Yard: A Conversation with Harun Farocki," in *Working on the Sight-Lines*, ed. Thomas Elsaesser (Amsterdam: Amsterdam University Press, 2004), 297–314, here 302.

36 See also David Tomas, *Vertov, Snow, Farocki: Machine Vision and the Posthuman* (New York: Bloomsbury Academic, 2013); and Oliver Müller, *Zwischen Mensch und Maschine: Vom Glück und Unglück des Homo faber* (Berlin: Suhrkamp, 2010).

37 Stressing the corporeal implications of Farocki's aesthetic strategy, Cowan astutely notes that Farocki's work is "addressed [...] to the human body. Where technological development has tended to exclude the body from the informational process, the installation format, by insisting on the physical act of viewing, makes spectators

aware of their bodily presence" (Cowan, "Rethinking the City Symphony," 85). In his discussion of Laura Poitras's work, Amir Eshel offers a wonderfully imaginative meditation on how "poetic thinking" might well take place "in the wake of the digital revolution" (Eshel, *Poetic Thinking Today: An Essay* [Stanford: Stanford University Press, 2020], 148).

38 See the third part of Farocki's *Eye/Machine.*

39 Farocki, "Contre-chant," 108.

40 Farocki, "Contre-chant," 107, translation modified; Farocki, "Tagebuch," 104.

41 Blüminger, "Memory and Montage," 103; Pantenburg, "*Gegen-Musik*," 98.

42 Farocki and Dziewior, "Gespräch," 222.

43 Farocki, *Bilderschatz*, 25; Farocki and Ernst, "Towards an Archive for Visual Concepts," 282.

44 Farocki, "Contre-chant," 108. Farocki writes: "[T]he most mundane activities are monitored by video. The images are not really intended to be watched. Only in exceptional cases are the tapes kept for further use and not erased" (Farocki, "Contre-chant," 108; see also Farocki, *Bilderschatz*, 25; Farocki and Ernst, "Towards an Archive for Visual Concepts," 282).

45 Farocki, *Bilderschatz*, 8; Farocki and Ernst, "Towards an Archive for Visual Concepts," 275.

46 See Winfried Pauleit, "Photographesomenon: Videoüberwachung und bildende Kunst," in *Bilder—Raum—Kontrolle: Videoüberwachung als Zeichen gesellschaftlichen Wandels*, ed. Leon Hempel and Jörg Metelmann (Frankfurt/M: Suhrkamp, 2005), 76–78. Pauleit writes: "The use of video surveillance produces a specific sort of image. In the present […] these usually stay invisible. […] Cameras are […] set up to double a specific spatio-temporal structure as an image trace that can be assessed retrospectively. A *second* reality is created as a security against unforeseen deviations. […] This production of images is directed towards a 'future perfect.' […] Deriving the name as an etymological transformation of 'photography' (light writing), I propose calling this type of image *photographesomenon* (light will have been written). The *photographesomenon* is already 'written,' even if it only constitutes itself as an image in futurity" (Pauleit, "Photographesomenon," 76–78, trans. as Pauleit, "Video Surveillance and Postmodern Subjects: The Effects of the Photographesomenon; An Image-Form in the 'Futur antérieur,'" in *Ctrl Space*, ed. Levin, Frohne, and Weibel, 465–79, here 469). On the prognostic force of surveillance, see also Jean Baudrillard, *Simulations*, trans. Paul Foss, Paul Patton, and Philip Beitchman (New York: Semiotext[e], 1983), 53–54.

47 See also Kammerer, *Bilder der Überwachung*, 157–58, 351.

48 Kammerer, *Bilder der Überwachung*, 157–58, 351.

49 Kammerer, *Bilder der Überwachung*, 320.

50 In Farocki's film *Prison Images* the narrator states: "The video images duplicate the control gaze. Their cold eye is intended to shed light on the prison, and so demystify it."

51 Kammerer, *Bilder der Überwachung*, 320.

52 Harun Farocki, "Kamera in Aufsicht," *Filmkritik* 27.9 (1983): 416–19, here 416.

53 Farocki, "Phantom Images," 18, emphasis mine.

54 Farocki, "Contre-chant," 108.

Works Cited

Alter, Nora. "The Political Im/perceptible in the Essay Film: Farocki's Images of the World and the Inscription of War." *New German Critique* 68 (1996): 165–92.

Barthes, Roland. *Mythologies*. Paris: Seuil, 1957.

Baudrillard, Jean. *Simulations*. Trans. Paul Foss, Paul Patton, and Philip Beitchman. New York: Semiotext[e], 1983.

Blüminger, Christa. "Memory and Montage: On the Installation *Counter-Music*." In *Harun Farocki: Against What? Against Whom?*, ed. Antje Ehmann and Kodwo Eshun, 101–9. London: Koenig Books, 2009.

Cowan, Michael. "Rethinking the City Symphony after the Age of Industry: Harun Farocki and the 'City Film.'" *Intermédialités: Histoire et théorie des arts, des lettres et des techniques* 11 (2008): 69–86.

Deleuze, Gilles. "Postscript on the Societies of Control." *October* 59 (1992): 3–7.

Dziewior, Yilmaz. "Harun Farocki: Weiche Montagen." In *Weiche Montagen/Soft Montages*, ed. Yilmaz Dziewior, 10–14. Cologne: Kunsthaus Bregenz, 2011.

Eshel, Amir. *Poetic Thinking Today: An Essay*. Stanford: Stanford University Press, 2020.

Farocki, Harun. *Bilderschatz*. Cologne: Buchhandlung Walther König, 1999.

Farocki, Harun. "Contre-chant." In *La ville qui fait signes*, ed. Alain Guiheux, 106–17. Paris: Éditions du Moniteur, 2004.

Farocki, Harun. "Controlling Observation." In *Harun Farocki: Imprint; Writings*, ed. Susanne Gaensheimer and Nicolaus Schafhausen, 306–21. New York: Lukas and Sternberg, 2001.

Farocki, Harun, dir. *Counter-Music*. Chicago, IL: Video Data Bank, 2004. DVD.

Farocki, Harun. "Cross Influence/Soft Montage." In *Harun Farocki: Against What? Against Whom?* ed. Antje Ehmann and Kodwo Eshun, 69–74. London: Koenig Books, 2009.

Farocki, Harun, dir. *I Thought I Was Seeing Convicts*. Chicago, IL: Video Data Bank, 2000. DVD.

Farocki, Harun. "Kamera in Aufsicht." *Filmkritik* 27 (1983): 416–19.

Farocki, Harun. "Phantom Images." *Public* 29 (2004): 12–24.

Farocki, Harun, dir. *Prison Images*. 2000; Berlin: Harun Farocki Filmproduktion, 2008. DVD.

Farocki, Harun. *Red Berta Goes Wandering without Love/Rote Berta geht ohne Liebe ander*. Cologne: Strzelecki Books, 2009.

Farocki, Harun. "Tagebuch: La ville qui fait signes." In *Weiche Montagen/Soft Montages*, ed. Yilmaz Dziewior, 104–8. Cologne: Kunsthaus Bregenz, 2011.

Farocki, Harun, dir. *War at a Distance*. 2003; Chicago, IL: Video Data Bank, 2004. DVD.

Farocki, Harun. "Written Trailers." In *Harun Farocki: Against What? Against Whom?* ed. Antje Ehmann and Kodwo Eshun, 220–41. London: Koenig Books, 2009.

Farocki, Harun, and Yilmaz Dziewior. "Gespräch, 23. Oktober 2010, Kunsthaus Bregenz." In *Weiche Montagen/Soft Montages*, ed. Yilmaz Dziewior, 204–26. Cologne: Kunsthaus Bregenz, 2011.

Farocki, Harun, and Wolfgang Ernst. "Towards an Archive for Visual Concepts." In *Working on the Sight-Lines*, ed. Thomas Elsaesser, 261–86. Amsterdam: Amsterdam University Press, 2004.

Farocki, Harun, and Rembert Hüser. "Nine Minutes in the Yard: A Conversation with Harun Farocki." In *Working on the Sight-Lines*, ed. Thomas Elsaesser, 297–314. Amsterdam: Amsterdam University Press, 2004.

Farocki, Harun, and Kaja Silverman. *Speaking about Godard*. New York: New York University Press, 1998.

Graham, Stephen. "Towards the Fifth Utility? On the Extension and Normalization of Public CCTV." In *Surveillance, Closed Circuit Television, and Social Control*, ed. Clive Norris, Jade Moran, and Gary Armstrong, 89–112. Brookfield, VT: Ashgate, 1989.

Haggerty, Kevin, and Richard Ericson. "The Surveillant Assemblage." *British Journal of Sociology* 41 (2000): 605–22.

Heidegger, Martin. "The Age of the World Picture." In *The Question Concerning Technology and Other Essays*, trans. William Lovitt, 129–30. New York: Harper and Row, 1982.

Hesiod. *The Homeric Hymns and Homerica.* Trans. Hugh G. Evelyn-White. Cambridge, MA: Harvard University Press, 1977.

Kammerer, Dietmar. *Bilder der Überwachung.* Frankfurt/M: Suhrkamp, 2008.

Keenan, Thomas. "Light Weapons." *Documents* 1–2 (1992): 147–58.

Lyon, David. *The Electronic Eye: The Rise of Surveillance Society.* Cambridge: Polity, 1994.

Lyon, David. *Surveillance Studies: An Overview.* Cambridge: Polity Press, 2007.

Müller, Oliver. *Zwischen Mensch und Maschine: Vom Glück und Unglück des Homo faber.* Berlin: Suhrkamp, 2010.

Pantenburg, Volker. *Film als Theorie: Bildforschung bei Harun Farocki und Jean-Luc Godard.* Bielefeld: Transcript, 2006.

Pantenburg, Volker. "*Gegen-Musik.*" In *Weiche Montagen/Soft Montages*, ed. Yilmaz Dziewior, 98–103. Cologne: Kunsthaus Bregenz, 2011.

Pauleit, Winfried. "Photographesomenon: Videoüberwachung und bildende Kunst." In *Bilder—Raum—Kontrolle: Videoüberwachung als Zeichen gesellschaftlichen Wandels*, ed. Leon Hempel and Jörg Metelmann, 76–78. Frankfurt/M: Suhrkamp, 2005.

Pauleit, Winfried. "Video Surveillance and Postmodern Subjects: The Effects of the Photographesomenon; an Image-Form in the 'Futur antérieur.'" In *Ctrl Space: Rhetorics of Surveillance from Bentham to Big Brother*, ed. Thomas Levin, Ursula Frohne, and Peter Weibel, 465–79. Cambridge, MA: MIT Press, 2002.

Simon, Bart. "The Return of Panopticism: Supervision, Subjection, and the New Surveillance." *Surveillance and Society* 3 (2005): 1–20.

Tomas, David. *Vertov, Snow, Farocki: Machine Vision and the Posthuman.* New York: Bloomsbury Academic, 2013.

Virilio, Paul. *The Vision Machine.* Bloomington, IN: Indiana University Press, 1994.

Westin, Alan F. *Privacy and Freedom.* New York: Atheneum, 1967.

Žižek, Slavoj. "Big Brother, or, the Triumph of the Gaze over the Eye." In *Ctrl Space: Rhetorics of Surveillance from Bentham to Big Brother*, ed. Thomas Levin, Ursula Frohne, and Peter Weibel, 224–27. Cambridge, MA: MIT Press, 2002.

2 Utterly Mysterious

Haneke's *Caché*

I

Since its premiere at the 2005 Cannes Film Festival, Michael Haneke's *Caché* has attracted an unusually broad critical reception. Many of these studies have, with good reason, focused on the theme of guilt, which permeates much of Haneke's oeuvre and figures prominently in *Caché*. Surprisingly few discussions have tackled the conspicuous presence of surveillance in the film, which we encounter right at its beginning and which, one might argue, imbues the film all the way to the last scene. This chapter focuses on surveillance and argues that Haneke's utterly mysterious film lends itself to a reading that relates the issues of guilt and surveillance. It conceives of guilt as enmeshed with surveillance and considers surveillance as inextricably linked with the notion of guilt. As such, Haneke's film confronts viewers with, and implicates them in, a quasi-religious experience that seems absent from much contemporary surveillance discourse but indeed lies at its core.

Caché opens with an establishing shot that directs our gaze to lush green bushes and ivy growing along the walls of a house, the townhouse, we soon learn, in which the film's protagonist, Georges Laurent, lives with his family. We hear the incessant chirping of sparrows, a sound that will return with the film's last shot,[1] and we follow the opening credits as they are inscribed onto the screen. There is much we cannot make out easily because the font is small and the letters appear only one by one. From the outset, there is an air of concealment, of secrecy, suffusing Haneke's film, a theme and a sensation that will pervade this picture from beginning to end. Even the street sign "Rue des Iris" on the house at the right margin of the screen appears strangely hidden, placed noticeably enough for us to make it out, but only upon second glance, and even then, the letters remain blurred.[2]

While initially the establishing shot has a strangely photographic feel to it for lack of movement, its filmic indexicality transpires when a man traverses the image from right to left. Two minutes into the film, a woman, whom we learn to be Anne, leaves the house, tightly pulling the entrance door and the porch gate behind her. We barely detect her, but Haneke's acoustic composition of banging

DOI: 10.4324/9781003229834-3

doors and clicking door latches ensures we do. We hear the cooing of pigeons, see a bicyclist cross the image from left corner back to right corner front, and only now, two and a half minutes into the film, are we given hints as to what to make of this first, excessively long long take in Haneke's film. We hear a man's voice, "Well?" and a woman's reply, "Nothing." "Where was it," asks the man: "In a plastic bag on the porch," responds the woman. As more pedestrians pass through the image, we hear the click of a door latch, the woman says, "What's wrong," we hear steps and another door opening; then a cut and the medium shot of a man, Georges, opening a third "door," the porch gate, and walking onto the street. The woman follows him at a distance, he turns and looks back at her, then crosses the street and stops, gazing down the street leading away from the house, perpendicular to our spectatorial gaze, and muses, "He must have been there." The man turns around to the woman, awaiting her response, but she only says, "Come inside." Both walk back into the house, and as we see him close the porch gate and the door to the house, and as we hear the click of the latch to the third door (which we soon learn divides the foyer from the living space), a conversation ensues about neighbors who may have witnessed something suspicious.

At this point, the image blurs and horizontal lines appear across the screen, indicating to us that what we are watching here is a surveillance tape now being forwarded. The woman says to the man, "The tape runs for over two hours," and the moment they and we identify Georges in the tape, apparently leaving the house in the morning to go to work, the tape is paused, rewound, and we now see in real time Georges crossing the street. The tape is paused again, and we see a freeze frame of Georges while hearing him cogitate, "How come I didn't see him? It'll remain a mystery." The woman suggests, "Maybe the camera was in the car," but the man, whom we soon will be introduced to as the host of a famous literature program on public television, refutes her hypothesis: "It doesn't look filmed through a window." As we see the main characters of Haneke's film, Georges and Anne, speculate about the origin of the tape—"Whose idea of a joke could this be?"—we realize that we have been spectators of the diegetic tape that they have viewed in their living room.[3] Haneke holds that information back from us for some time and "hides" it along with much that is "hidden" in this film.[4] In fact, the tastefully decorated townhouse of this affluent Parisian couple and their twelve-year-old pubertal son appears strangely hidden. There is virtually no window that would allow the outside world to peek in; instead, layers and layers of boundaries hide it, beginning with a white dwarf wall, high green bushes, and a fence, then a porch that leads to the townhouse's receded entrance, which in turn is separated by a foyer from the living room. The relevance of this multilayered separation between the public or outside and the private or inside has everything to do with the tape, which shows nothing and yet comes as a shock to the couple. It literally shows the outside facade of their house, but it signifies that they are under surveillance, that some outside gaze threatens their well-protected private domain. The combination of the protecting bushes and fence and the acoustically accentuated presence of the gate and two doors invoke a fortress,[5] or a prison, a sense emphasized by Georges's and Anne's baggy nondescript clothes, hers gray and his beige.[6] Combine this with the surveillant gaze that sees them while remaining unseen, and a prototypical panoptic setup presents itself.[7] No doubt, Georges and Anne are not literally prisoners, they don't literally live in a prison, and there is no prison guard monitoring them from a central watchtower. At the same time, the Benthamite panopticon served its most famous interpreter, Michel Foucault, as the framework for the theorization of a much more encompassing disciplinary gaze that Foucault saw as characterizing modern society itself.[8] We shall return to Haneke's evocation of a disciplinary surveillant gaze and its effect of internalization on the surveilled.

II

At this point, it is helpful to simply acknowledge the ubiquity of moments of surveillance throughout the film. Shortly after the viewing of the tape, Georges muses whether a friend of their son, Pierrot, might have made the tape to play "games on his pal's bobo parents." When Georges asks Anne about Pierrot's whereabouts, and she replies that "he'll be home soon," we are presented with a form of parental surveillance that will imbue the film from beginning to end, not least in its failings. A similar form of parental surveillance appears when Georges visits his elderly mother, who is not deceived by his formulaic chitchat and intuits that something weighs on his mind.[9] The Laurent family's dinner includes Georges's inquisitive questioning of Pierrot, which epitomizes a kind of disciplinary surveillance.[10] Another such case of disciplinary surveillance presents itself with Pierrot's swimming lesson and the piercing instructions that the coach directs at his students. At a swim meet, later in the film, audience members equipped with video cameras monitor the competing children.[11] An instance of disciplinary surveillance occurs when Georges picks Pierrot up from school and Pierrot mentions that his teacher disapproves of Georges's sending him cards at school. We encounter a form of surveillance that Friedrich Schiller famously described as the "eye of the law" when Georges and Anne go to the police and, later in the film, when the police arrest Majid and his son, take them to the police station, and incarcerate them there.[12] A softer form of surveillance, which Gilles Deleuze, in his radicalized reading of Foucault, termed "societies of control," arises with the relations Anne and Georges maintain vis-à-vis their respective employers.[13] Specifically, we are presented with a form of work surveillance as Georges is summoned by his boss about the tape the latter received and the threat that its content might pose to Georges's career should it end up "in the wrong hands."[14] Georges's job itself, of course, epitomizes a form of synoptic surveillance, in which it is no longer the *one* (guard) watching the *many* (inmates) but wherein *many* TV spectators watch *one* famous TV host, Georges Laurent, in his biweekly literary talk show.[15] There are numerous moments where surveillance appears in its most basic version as someone watching

Figure 2.1 *Caché* (Michael Haneke, 2005).

someone else who cannot reciprocate the gaze. Consider Anne and Pierre's romantically charged conversation at a coffee shop that seems not so inconspicuously overheard by another customer in the back of the image. Think of Georges sitting in a convenience shop drinking coffee from a plastic cup and monitoring the house that he is about to enter so as to confront the putative originator of the tapes. Our spectatorial gaze shifts back and forth here between Georges's surveillant gaze, which we intermittently assume, and a medium shot showing Georges in the act of surveillance. Or, toward the end of the film, Georges as he—in a classical surveillance cinema position—hides behind the bedroom's window curtain upstairs and observes Anne's guests as they leave the house and walk down the street at night (Figures 2.1 and 2.2).[16]

Figure 2.2 *Caché* (Michael Haneke, 2005).

Figure 2.3 *Caché* (Michael Haneke, 2005).

We see, via a point-of-view shot, *with* the surveillor and then look *at* him: we surveil the surveillor, as it were. The darkness of the night saturated by the bright light of street lamps evokes in itself a form of surveillance that became prevalent when Louis XIV, the Roi-Soleil, ordered street lights to be installed across the streets of Paris so that every mischief, even at night, would be seeable and hence punishable.[17] "The [...] shadowless light," historian Wolfgang Schivelbusch notes, "no longer guarantees the security of the individual. It permits total surveillance by the state. The Utopian dream of nights lit up as bright as day was transformed into the nightmare of a light from which there was no escape."[18] With the ubiquitous installation of street lamps, night was turned into day, and no room for escape from the all-seeing, omniscient, and omnipotent gaze of state power remained. The ornate lights illuminating the streets in *Caché* are an emblem of that urban form of surveillance (Figure 2.3).[19]

All these concrete and often discrete moments of surveillance notwithstanding, the most pervasive form of surveillance, for us as cinematic spectators and certainly for Georges as protagonist, is the video surveillance captured on the anonymously sent tapes. Of course, what motivates much of Haneke's psychological thriller is the question of "Whodunnit?"[20] And of course, that question leads nowhere insofar as technically the tape shown at the film's beginning cannot exist—Georges would have seen whoever recorded him when he left the house. It is an impossibility for the tape to exist or, as Georges mutters, it is utterly "mysterious": "How come I didn't see him? It'll remain a mystery." While the tape, on some epistemic level, cannot be,[21] the notion of a gaze that is distinctly perceived without its source being identifiable, of course, is a commonplace in the history of ideas and has long been associated with the omniscient and omnipresent gaze of God. This is a gaze that, traditionally, is at times perceived as a threat and, at times, as promising protection.[22] The ambiguity of God's gaze signifying control but also care crucially constitutes its force and extends to much of modern-day surveillance technology.[23] Georges Laurent clearly perceives the surveillance he is under as a threat. Before long, it triggers in him a bad conscience and, indeed, gives rise to a distinct sense of guilt that ultimately lies at the center of Haneke's film.[24]

III

Georges's individual feelings of guilt and the bad conscience from which he suffers cannot be separated from a more collective dimension of guilt.[25] It is here that the film's postcolonial backdrop comes into play, for Georges, of course, represents a history of oppressors and colonizers who colonized, controlled, and, in fact, surveilled the very Algerian subject who now, figuratively, returns the surveillant gaze.[26] To be sure, it is not particularly significant in this context that Georges betrayed the child Majid and had him effectively expelled from the family farm, an act of childhood jealousy and aggression that does not amount to any particular individualized guilt for Georges, who, after all, was a child and, as such, morally not fully capable and accountable.[27] It does, however, underscore Georges's involvement in the collective history of colonial whiteness from which he has benefited and continues to benefit in ways Majid has and does not.[28] Georges's guilt lies in the failure to acknowledge that systemic injustice, in his ongoing denial or unwillingness to respond to it adequately. And so, there is a certain irony in the fact that the colonial subject, traditionally subjected to the controlling gaze of the oppressor, now appears to gaze back. And it does not actually matter whether the videotapes come from Majid or not. What distinguishes *Caché* from much surveillance cinema is that it focuses less on the watcher and more on the watched,[29] on the psychological effect that surveillance precipitates in the watched, that is, the guilty conscience triggered in Georges.[30]

The linkage between surveillance and Georges's mental state—that is, the extent to which the tapes are projections,[31] articulations of internalized guilt—is not clear at the outset. Tape One presents Georges's life from an outside perspective—we see him leave for work in the morning, see his wife leave for work, and see the house they live in. The tape is identifiable as a surveillance tape by the horizontal lines across the screen when the tape is eventually rewound in conjunction with the Laurents' voice-over commentary. Tape Two resembles Tape One in that it shows the comings and goings of the Laurent family; it is similarly marked as a surveillance video by horizontal lines upon rewinding, but shot at night this time, and, importantly, interspersed with Georges's mental images. We see, for the blink of an eye, the intercut close-up of a boy who is bleeding from his mouth—resonating with the drawing sent along with the tape[32]—and soon identified by us as the boy Majid. This is the first instance of a moment where the perspective invoked in a surveillance tape is associated with Georges's perspective, specifically his childhood experiences.

Tape Three arrives in the middle of a dinner party: the doorbell rings and Georges gets up to open, but there is no one at the door, only the empty street in front of the house, cloaked in darkness. Georges feels as if he is being watched, but he cannot make out who or what is watching him. The feeling of powerlessness is, not least, precipitated by the camerawork here. First, we see, through a point-of-view shot, the empty street outside the house to the left, masked in darkness and captured in a long take. Then the image cuts to a shot depicting the resigned Georges in medium close-up, and a moment later it cuts to yet another point-of-view shot, this time of the empty street to his right, again captured as a long take. Corresponding to the paradoxical dynamic of surveillance—seeing without being seen—Georges's frustration results not from a particular discomforting instance to which he could attribute his sense of being powerless but rather from the very fact of not being able to identify anything at all: "What's this all about? Show yourself, you coward! Show yourself and say what you want!" Of course, this desire to confront and challenge the surveilling authority must remain unanswered. Georges shouts and demands of the person who rang the bell to drop the disguise, but rather than receive a reply he notices, as he returns into the house, a tape placed on the doorsill. He cannot close the door because the tape is blocking the way, and the fact that the tape lies on that threshold without having been there when Georges stepped out of the house or without having been placed there in the meantime amounts to no less than another ontological impossibility. While it seems diegetically illogical or "mysterious" for the tape to be where it is, the drawing sent with the tape provides another lead to Georges's childhood. We see a rooster whose head is severed and which is drenched in blood, an image we soon learn to place in relation to Majid, Georges's childhood nemesis. The tape's footage further advances the film's narrative: we look through the rain-covered windshield of a car with running wipers driving down a country road.[33] The car stops, and the hand-held camera abruptly pans to the left and focuses on a country house, the house Georges grew up in, his parents' estate, which his mother still inhabits. We see, one might say, the ground zero of Georges's guilt. While the camera surreptitiously records the country house, the contiguity between surveillance and Georges's mental life is tight here, and it is not by chance that the scene jump-cuts to a shot displaying Georges sitting on the bed of his elderly mother, to whom he pays a visit.

The fourth anonymously sent tape arriving at the Laurent household does not strictly qualify as surveillance—it shows a car ride through Paris and leads the way down a long murky hallway to Majid's low-rent apartment. Information is not so much gathered here as exhibited for Georges to act on, and it is important to acknowledge that the linkage between surveillance and Georges's mind is not consistent—Haneke's film is imbued with poetic ambiguities and open ends that defy systemization. Tape Four does, however, underscore the convergence of the tape's perspective and Georges's perspective, for moments later Georges will walk down that very same hallway, adopting the exact same perspective assumed in the tape.[34] With the fifth tape, the convergence between surveillance and Georges's mind reaches its pinnacle. Following the lead adumbrated in Tape Four, Georges visits Majid at his apartment. We witness an increasingly contentious conversation between Majid and Georges. The camerawork and editing follow familiar feature-film patterns: there is a series of shot-reverse shots aligned with high-angle/low-angle shots, establishing Georges (via low angle shots) as powerful and Majid (via high angle shots) as disempowered and markedly gentle. In contrast to Haneke's characteristic long-take cinematography, we perceive frequent cuts combined with a series of pan and tilt shots that ensure that the action appears fluid. The relevance of this rather unspectacular employment of continuity editing becomes apparent with the surfacing of the surveillance tape of the exchange that Anne, and with her we, Haneke's spectators, will come to watch moments later. At that point, we witness the conversation between Georges and Majid a second time, but this time through the eye of a surveillance camera that appears to have recorded the interaction surreptitiously along with Majid's subsequent crying fit. What characterizes this footage as surveillance—beyond comments by Anne and later Georges's boss regarding the tape—is its specific indexicality: the second time around there are no pans or tilts, and there are no shot-reverse shots or any cuts for that matter. Camerawork and editing shift from the style of a feature film to the style of surveillance footage, which never seeks to evoke any particular meaning or intention. The naked eye of the surveillance camera merely records. It does not care about our affective involvement or spectatorial response but solely registers.[35] Combine this with the impossibility of locating the surveillance camera in Majid's apartment—even careful scrutiny reveals no position where the camera might have been set up. How to read this surveillance tape, whose perspective seems so perfectly aligned with Georges's perspective, other than as a metonymy of Georges' mind? The surveillance camera functions as an enactment of Georges Laurent's mental state and perhaps his suppressed feelings of guilt as he berates Majid in his apartment, accuses and threatens him, all while reinscribing the traditional roles of aggressor and aggressed-upon, oppressor and oppressed, colonizer and colonized.

IV

While the nexus between surveillance and Georges's mind discussed thus far pertains mostly to unambiguous instances of surveillance footage, there are myriad shots in the film that defy easy classification as surveillance while mobilizing a certain surveillant image economy. Consider the many stationary shots in *Caché* that carry the same wide-frame and long-take signature as the surveillance shots but are not confirmed diegetically *as* surveillance.[36] An example is the scene when Georges, following Majid's suicide, steps out of a movie theater, captured in a static frame via a long take that does not direct any focus at him through close-ups or pans but instead seems to capture him on tape by mere happenstance.[37] How about the barn scene where we witness Majid beheading a rooster (that national symbol of France), an event silently observed by the child Georges? We see a rooster that is held down on a block of wood and then an ax that abruptly cuts off its head.[38] The camerawork in this dream sequence is curious in its own way insofar as Majid beheads the rooster with an ax and then ominously moves toward Georges with that ax in his hands—a perceived threat that Georges seems to construct in order to self-justify his tattling on Majid's alleged wrongdoings. Notably, while we first watch the beheading of the rooster from Georges's surveillant perspective, the film then cuts to Majid's perspective as he slowly walks toward Georges—a diegetic distortion that makes a lot of sense if one assumes that Georges really "writes" the storyline here and imputes these acts to Majid. What solidifies is precisely the aforementioned nexus between Georges's surveillant perspective and his psyche or mind. Georges constructs his dream, as it were, in such a way that Majid must have posed a danger to him and thus rightly was sent off to an orphanage. Even in his dreams, Georges "directs" the story in a way that suits him—mechanisms of denial and suppression are fully operative.

A similar surveillant image economy transpires with the second dream scene set at the barn, captured again as a stationary shot with that same wide-frame and long-take cinematography. We again adopt Georges's perspective as he, out of the barn, clandestinely observes Majid's "deportation" from the Laurent estate to an orphanage: we see the idyllic courtyard with roaming chickens, a green car drives up to the house, a man and a woman step out who have come to pick up Majid. Majid tries to run away but is caught and forcibly dragged into the car, screaming all the way. The visual composition of this scene is again noteworthy: we follow these gut-wrenching images from a seemingly hidden perspective—presumably from the point of view of young Georges who is hiding in the barn and monitoring Majid's removal. The lower third of the image is covered in darkness, the shade of the barn, whereas Majid's struggle is placed in the sun-flooded courtyard (Figure 2.4). Young Georges sees without being seen, tacitly monitoring the cruel spectacle. Because adult Georges's bad conscience is rooted precisely in this moment—Majid's expulsion to an orphanage, which he, Georges, has initiated—it seems safe to say that this shot late in the film is the catalyst behind the tapes that arrive at the Laurents' house. In other words, it is always Georges who is surveilling, whose internalized guilt keeps him in a distressed reflex of self-monitoring. What we see in those tapes is, on some level, always Georges's guilt-ridden self-observation.

Figure 2.4 *Caché* (Michael Haneke, 2005).

The surveillant image economy of *Caché* extends all the way to the final scene depicting Pierrot's school and, seemingly fortuitously, capturing the conversation between Pierrot and Majid's son in the left margin of the frame. If the film's first shot initially appears as filmic narrative and only subsequently presents itself as film within the film, as surveillance tape watched by diegetic characters, then such clearly marked separation between Haneke's film and surveillance tapes within the film's diegesis appears increasingly hard to make out, so much so that the enigmatic final shot echoes the film's first shot in cinematography (long take, wide static frame) while lacking any concrete indication of its being or not being surveillance footage. No doubt, the destabilization of mediatic boundaries between diegetic surveillance tapes and filmic narrative[39] involves us as spectators, who, just like Georges, watch these images and who, just like Georges, are called upon, indeed pressed, to respond and to conjure up a sense of responsibility for that history of colonial violence in which we most likely partake, not directly as agents but perhaps as beneficiaries.[40] What emerges here is Haneke's view according to which we all live in a state of guilt, his characters as much as we, his spectators, and it is incumbent on us to account for this guilt and respond to it.[41] Any reading of the film that attempts to solve the question of "Whodunnit?" misses that larger underlying etiological conception of history embraced by Haneke (one that Walter Benjamin captured beautifully when writing, "Guilt is the highest category of world history [...]. A state of the world is [...] always guilty with regard to some other later one").[42] *Caché* is surveillance cinema conceived at a time of ubiquitous surveillance that forces us back into the experience of guilt-ridden subjects observed and self-observing in light of the power-political atrocities we are embroiled in and entangled with. While Georges does not realize this entanglement and ensuing responsibility, Haneke's film provides an imaginative space in which to experience and account for a reality that is ours to reckon with.

Notes

1 Michel Chion, "Without Music: On *Caché*," in *A Companion to Michael Haneke*, ed. Roy Grundmann (Malden, MA: Wiley-Blackwell, 2010), 161–67, here 167.

2 Elizabeth Ezra and Jane Sillars put forth a mythological reading of the street sign "Rue des Iris" with reference to the goddess Iris in "*Hidden* in Plain Sight: Bringing Terror Home," *Screen* 48.2 (2007): 215–21, here 218–19. For a suggestive discussion of the name of the street in light of the film's postcolonial frame of reference, see Mohit Chandna, "Out of Place: French Family at (Algerian) War," in *Spatial Boundaries, Abounding Spaces: Colonial Borders in French and Francophone Literature and Film* (Leuven: Leuven University Press, 2021), 205–37, here 226.

3 The opening of *Caché* has given rise to myriad analyses; mention should be made of Garrett Stewart, *Framed Time: Toward a Postfilmic Cinema* (Chicago: University of Chicago Press, 2007), 195–96; Martin Seel, *The Arts of Cinema* (Ithaca: Cornell University Press, 2018), 121–22; Thomas Y. Levin, "Five Tapes, Four Halls, Two Dreams: Vicissitudes of Surveillant Narration in Michael Haneke's *Caché*," in *A Companion to Michael Haneke*, ed. Grundmann, 75–90, here 76; Ipek A. Celik, *In Permanent Crisis: Ethnicity in Contemporary European Media and Cinema* (Ann Arbor: University of Michigan Press, 2015), 53–75, here 61; Thomas Elsaesser, "Performative Self-Contradictions: Michael Haneke's Mind Games," in *A Companion to Michael Haneke*, ed. Grundmann, 53–74, here 64–65; Saige Walton, *Cinema's Baroque Flesh: Film, Phenomenology and the Art of Entanglement* (Amsterdam: Amsterdam University Press, 2016), 66–68; Lutz Koepnick, *The Long Take: Art Cinema and the Wondrous* (Minneapolis: University of Minnesota Press, 2017), 142–43; Sulgie Lie, *Towards a Political Aesthetics of Cinema: The Outside of Film* (Amsterdam: Amsterdam University Press, 2020), 151–53; Susanne Kaul, *Michael Haneke: Einführung in seine Filme und Filmästhetik* (Paderborn: Wilhelm Fink Verlag, 2018), 138–39.

4 "Hidden" aspects in *Caché* include, of course, Georges's suppressed childhood relationship with Majid that haunts him into adulthood, even though he repeatedly insists that he has "nothing to hide" ("Je n'ai rien à cacher"). See *Caché (Hidden)*, directed by Michael Haneke (2004; Culver City, CA: Sony Pictures Home Entertainment, 2006), DVD. Georges's "hidden" relationship to Majid, in turn, allegorically reflects France's suppressed relationship to its colonial past, its repressed guilt, and specifically the events of October 17, 1961. (On *Caché*'s partaking in "recent reflection on the long-repressed events of October 17, 1961," see Michael Rothberg, *Multidirectional Memory: Remembering the Holocaust in the Age of Decolonization* [Stanford: Stanford University Press, 2009], 270–98, here 281). Curiously, while the film was released under the title *Hidden* in the U.K., the U.S. release appeared under the original French title, *Caché*. And the French word *caché* indeed carries a connotation that gets lost with the translation "hidden," namely, a sense of intentionality, of something being deliberately kept secret. (Regarding the semantic polyvalence of the title *Caché*, see Asbjørn Grønstad, *Screening the Unwatchable: Spaces of Negation in Post-Millennial Art Cinema* [London: Palgrave, 2012], 150–62, here 156–57.) Of course, the sender of the tapes remains hidden as well and, for that very reason, appears so ominous. In this context, the allusion to an authority or entity that exerts control while staying unidentifiable might be evocative of the unseen and unknown yet omnipresent and omniscient gaze of God.

5 See Michael Cowan, "Between the Street and the Apartment: Disturbing the Space of Fortress Europe in Michael Haneke," *Studies in European Cinema* 5.2 (2008): 117–29, here especially 117 and 123–24.

6 The first commentators to have invoked the prison metaphor with respect to the Laurents' house and domestic life are, to my knowledge, Ezra and Sillars, "*Hidden* in Plain Sight," 216.

7 See Jeremy Bentham, *The Panopticon Writings* (London: Verso, 1995), 43.

8 Foucault describes the panopticon as an "important mechanism" that "automatizes and disindividualizes power. Power," he elaborates, "has its principle not so much in a person as [. . .] in an arrangement whose internal mechanisms produce the relation in which individuals are caught up" (Michel Foucault, *Discipline and Punish: The Birth of the Prison* [New York: Vintage Books, 1977], 202; see also 216). On the ways in which *Caché* resonates with Foucault's theorization of the panopticon, see Jennifer Burris, "Surveillance and the Indifferent Gaze in Michael Haneke's *Caché*," *Studies in French Cinema* 11.2 (2011): 151–63, here 152–53, 157–58; Andrea Gogröf-Voorhees, "Surveillance and Voyeurism in Haneke's *Code Unknown* and *Caché*," in *Fascinatingly Disturbing: Interdisciplinary Perspectives on Michael Haneke's Cinema* (Eugene, OR: Pickwick, 2010), 259–81, here 264–66; Levin, "Five Tapes, Four Halls, Two Dreams," 75; Susana Araujo, "Inhospitality, Security, and the Global 'Homeland' in Michael Haneke's *Caché*," in *Security and Hospitality in Literature and Culture: Modern and Contemporary Perspectives*, ed. Jeffrey Clapp and Emily Ridge (New York: Routledge, 2016), 243–57, here 249; Todd Herzog, "The Banality of Surveillance: Michael Haneke's *Caché* and Life after the End of Privacy," *Modern Austrian Literature* 43.2 (2010): 25–40, here 37.

9 Because Georges's mother doesn't buy into Georges's pretty talk, because she senses that he is hiding something, she looks apathetically at him, as if ready to end the conversation. He gives it another attempt, this time accusing *her* of hiding something: "But I get the feeling you're not fine," a sorry attempt that she instantly brushes off: "You seem strange, Georges. Listening to you, I'm worried about you. What's going on?" Georges shows himself surprised, plays her for a fool, but there seems no way to fool his mother, who can virtually look through him, can read his every thought or at least pick up on his anxiety. She adopts, in the language of surveillance, the traditional role of the surveilling parent here, who knows and sees everything in a typically ambivalent role of "care and control" (David Lyon, *Surveillance Studies: An Overview* [Cambridge: Polity Press, 2007], 3). The surveillant authority that Georges seeks to eschew returns, as it were, in the form of his mother. The feeling of guilt triggered by the tapes that he had hoped to shed in conversation with his mother returns to be reinforced in the face of his mother, who functions as the image of divine authority. And because it is the old, bedridden, frail mother who embodies authority here and assumes control, she changes the topic and figuratively sends him on his way: "When are you leaving?" This conversation, shot as a series of shot-reverse shots, systematically oscillates between low- and high-angle shots, in which the old mother is shown in depowering high-angle shots, whereas Georges is depicted in empowering low-angle shots. And yet, this presentational register, consistent as it may be with Georges's assumption that he is the one in charge, is at odds with the filmic narrative, wherein Georges appears as the child seeking approval from his mother. Put differently, while the scene's visual enactment is aligned with Georges's reasoning, the narrative of *Caché* does not succumb to this logic at all but rather undermines or challenges it. Georges wants to be in control and yet continuously realizes that he is controlled by forces watching "over" and "after" him, by a surveillant force that has always been there and from which there seems no escape (Lyon, *Surveillance Studies*, 3).

10 See Foucault, *Discipline and Punish*, especially 135–230

11 On the mediatic "competition" between film and video in this scene, see Eric Cazdyn, *The Already Dead: The New Time of Politics, Culture, and Illness* (Durham: Duke University Press, 2012), 40–41; see also Lie, *Towards a Political Aesthetics of Cinema*, 153–54.

12 Friedrich Schiller, "The Song of the Bell," in *The Poems of Friedrich Schiller*, ed. and trans. E. P. Arnold-Foster (New York: Henry Holt, 1902), 246–59, here 255. For a thoughtful discussion of the metaphor of the "eye of the law," see Michael Stolleis, *The Eye of the Law: Two Essays on Legal History* (New York: Routledge, 2009), 1–13. If the eye of God figures, in a secular context, as the "eye of the law," then the police, as the executive arm of the law, embody the authority that is to guarantee compliance with the law. Going to the police corresponds in this respect with turning to God, whose watchful gaze, again, signifies control but also care (see Lyon, *Surveillance Studies*, 3). The ambiguity is characteristic of the scene because, on the one hand, Georges sees himself as a victim and seeks protection *through* the police, but, on the other hand, he has been avoiding the controlling authority *of* the police, at least at first.

13 Gilles Deleuze, "Postscript on the Societies of Control," *October* 59 (1992): 3–7.

14 See Elia Zureik, "Theorizing Surveillance: The Case of the Workplace," in *Surveillance as Social Sorting*, ed. David Lyon (London: Routledge, 2003), 31–56.

15 I adopt the concept of synoptic surveillance from Norwegian sociologist Thomas Mathiesen's pathbreaking article, "The Viewer Society: Michel Foucault's Panopticon Revisited." Whereas the Benthamite/Foucauldian panopticon allows "the few" to watch "the many," Mathiesen's notion of the "synopticon"—typified distinctly by mass media, above all television—enables "the many [...] to see [...] the few." Needless to say, and as Mathiesen himself stresses, the two notions are not to be thought of as diametrically opposed but as coexisting and inextricably linked ("The Viewer Society: Michel Foucault's Panopticon Revisited," *Theoretical Criminology* 1.2 [1997]: 215–34, here 215).

16 Georges asks Anne what she said to the guests to make them leave early. She says she lied when taking his phone call earlier—claiming it was an anonymous caller—and explains that she lied because Georges had a problem and needed to talk to her. The fact that even those who help others have to "lie" to be able to provide assistance shows how all-encompassing Haneke's understanding of "lying" is and how inescapable the spell of guilt is in his view. There is a certain irony in the fact that Georges, who lies constantly, sounds downright unbelievable at the moment he is telling the truth. Anne: "What happened?" Georges: "It's like I told you. I arrived. He asked me in and killed himself. There was a lot of blood." This is all the more ironic because he immediately follows with another lie. Asked where he was between the incident around four in the afternoon and his arrival home, he claims, "Nowhere. In town." We, of course, know that he was at the movies, but Georges knows that going to the movies (immersing himself in alternate realities) rather than the police (thereby risking his immediate arrest) would cast a bad light on him. And so, he lies, is perhaps forced to lie—that is the point here: the liar is not necessarily an intentional evildoer. Rather, guilt is the medium within which we live and act; it is, if you will, the very matrix of being human.

17 See Dietmar Kammerer, *Bilder der Überwachung* (Frankfurt/M: Suhrkamp Verlag, 2008), 20. David Lyon writes: "Ever since the fabled Tower of Babel and the related urban space of Babylon, the city has been the site of numerous experiments in political-economic aggrandizement and social engineering. [...] As public lighting became technically feasible in early modern cities, so the idea of being visible in urban space was more connected with social control. Paris was perhaps the first 'city of light' when police chief Nicolas de la Reynie installed thousands of lanterns at the end of the seventeenth century. By the end of the twentieth century,

however, many cities had helped to bring about the reversal of the Roman ideal. No longer did citizens merely see and comply with the architectural demands of urban space; the urban spaces were themselves enabled to see the citizens, as it were, courtesy of CCTV" (Lyon, *Surveillance Studies*, 37). See also Pete Fussey and Jon Coaffee, "Urban Spaces of Surveillance," in *Routledge Handbook of Surveillance Studies*, ed. Kirstie Ball et al. (New York: Routledge, 2012), 201–8.

18 Wolfgang Schivelbusch, *Disenchanted Night: The Industrialization of Light in the Nineteenth Century* (Berkeley: University of California Press, 1995), 134; see also Kammerer, *Bilder der Überwachung*, 22; Jonathan Crary, *24/7: Late Capitalism and the Ends of Sleep* (London: Verso, 2013), 16–17.

19 This type of surveillance is dealt with in some detail in Harun Farocki's installation *Counter-Music*, where surveillance by street lamps is imagistically intertwined with surveillance by video cameras, that is, integrated into one and the same image.

20 To be sure, Haneke deems the question of "Whodunnit?" to be ultimately misled: "If you think it's Majid, Pierrot, Georges, the malevolent director, God himself, the human conscience—all these answers are correct. But if you come out wanting to know who sent the tapes, you didn't understand the film. To ask this question is to avoid asking the real question the film raises, which is more: how do we treat our conscience and our guilt and reconcile ourselves to living with our actions? People are only asking, 'whodunnit?' because I chose to use the genre, the structure of a thriller, to address the issues of blame and conscience, and these methods of narrative usually demand an answer. But my film isn't a thriller and who am I to presume to give anyone an answer on how they should deal with their own guilty conscience?" (Michael Haneke, quoted in Jason Solomons, "We Love Hidden. But What Does It Mean?" *The Guardian*, February 18, 2006).

21 On the metaphoricity of the surveillance tapes, see Garrett Stewart, *Closed Circuits: Screening Narrative Surveillance* (Chicago: University of Chicago Press, 2015), 156 and 166; Catherine Zimmer, *Surveillance Cinema* (New York: New York University Press, 2015), 63–64.

22 In the Bible, God's gaze figures as equally caring and controlling, as simultaneously protective and threatening (see Kammerer, *Bilder der Überwachung*, 227–28). Consider, for example, Zechariah 4:10: "For who hath despised the day of small things? for they shall rejoice, and shall see the plummet in the hand of Zerubbabel with those seven; they are the eyes of the LORD, which run to and fro through the whole earth." This menacing side of God appears intimately related to expressly shielding traits: "For the eyes of the LORD run to and fro throughout the whole earth, to shew himself strong in the behalf of them whose heart is perfect toward him" (2 Chronicles 16:9).

23 See Lyon, *Surveillance Studies*, 3. "Surveillance practices are probably basic to human society and start with any elementary watching of some by another in order to create an effect of looking *after* or looking *over* the latter," David Lyon writes. It goes without saying that the seeming antipodes of "care and control" are not to be thought of in merely dichotomic terms but may well inform each other (3). See also Kammerer, *Bilder der Überwachung*, 104–5, 227–28; Hartmut Böhme, *Natur und Subjekt* (Frankfurt/M: Suhrkamp Verlag, 1988), 238–39. Cf. Stolleis, *The Eye of the Law*, 5.

24 My invoking of the biblical tradition here distinguishes itself from the many readings of *Caché* that employ a distinctly psychoanalytic register. See, for instance, Catherine Wheatley, *Michael Haneke's Cinema: The Ethics of the Image* (New York: Berghahn Books, 2009), 184; Lie, *Towards a Political Aesthetics of Cinema*, 162; Rina Dudai, "Trauma in Translation: Crossing the Boundaries between Psychoanalysis and Film," *Projections: The Journal for Movies and Mind* 8.1 (2014): 41–60, here 49; Margarete Johanna Landwehr, "Voyeurism, Violence, and

the Power of the Media: The Reader's/Spectator's Complicity in Jelinek's *The Piano Teacher* and Haneke's *La Pianiste, Caché, The White Ribbon,*" *International Journal of Applied Psychoanalytic Studies* 8.2 (2011): 117–32, here 125; Stephen Humphreys, "Conscience in the Datasphere," *Humanity* 6.3 (2015): 361–86, here 371–72; Hugh S. Manon, "Comment ça rien? Screening the Gaze in *Caché*," in *On Michael Haneke*, ed. Brian Price and John David Rhodes (Detroit: Wayne State University Press, 2010), 105–25, here 121–23; James Penney, "'You Never Look at Me from Where I See You': Postcolonial Guilt in *Caché*," *New Formations* 70 (2010): 77–93, here 91–93; Frances L. Restuccia, "The Virtue of Blushing: Assimilating Anxiety into Shame in Haneke's *Caché*," *Symplokē* 18 (2010): 155–70.

25 It is in this context that we must consider the incessantly intercut world news on the television in the Laurent household about violence in Iraq, the West's "engagement" in the Middle East, and so forth. This mise en abyme presents a configuration of guilt situated on a collective, societal level, which Haneke parses and places in ambiguous relation to the questions of individual guilt of the film's protagonist, Georges Laurent. On the multifarious inclusion of news coverage in *Caché*, see Stewart, *Closed Circuits*, 166; Burris, "Surveillance and the Indifferent Gaze," 161; T. Jefferson Kline, "The Intertextual and Discursive Origins of Terror in Michael Haneke's *Caché*," in *A Companion to Michael Haneke*, ed. Grundmann, 551–61, here 556–58; Patrick O'Donnell, "Frame-Up: James, *Caché*, and the Borders of the Visible," *New Centennial Review* 13.2 (2013): 223–38, here 235; Eva Jorholt, "White Paranoia: Michael Haneke's *Caché* Reflected through Alain Robbe-Grillet's Novel *La Jalousie*," *Studies in French Cinema* 17 (2017): 91–108, here 105–6.

26 "The theme of surveillance is [...] relevant to the colonial history that forms the background of *Caché*," Michael Rothberg writes. "Already in the middle of the nineteenth century, as Alexis de Tocqueville's 1847 'Rapport sur l'Algérie' demonstrates, French colonialism in Algeria was driven by the desire to *'put under surveillance' the Algerian people, so as to 'penetrate their techniques, their ideas, their beliefs, and [...] the secret to governing them*'" (*Multidirectional Memory*, 358n15; emphasis mine).

27 "[I]n Kantian terms," Catherine Wheatley reminds us, "a child exists in the ethical state of nature: it is only when they reach adulthood that they come to understand the morality of their desires and actions and therefore assume responsibility for them" (*Michael Haneke's Cinema*, 164). See also Christopher Rowe, *Michael Haneke: The Intermedial Void* (Evanston: Northwestern University Press, 2017), 175.

28 See also Ezra and Sillars, "*Hidden* in Plain Sight," 219. Numerous commentators have pointed out how the individual story of guilt epitomized by Georges intersects with France's collective story of guilt. See Walton, *Cinema's Baroque Flesh*, 66; Jehanne-Marie Gavarini, "Rewind: The Will to Remember, the Will to Forget in Michael Haneke's *Caché*," in *Millennial Cinema: Memory in Global Film*, ed. Amresh Sinha and Terence McSweeney (New York: Wallflower Press, 2011), 192–208, here 205–6; Rothberg, *Multidirectional Memory*, 270–98, here 283; Justice McGill, "Bad Memories: Haneke with Locke on Personal Identity and Post-Colonial Guilt," *Film-Philosophy* 17.1 (2013): 134–53, here 141; Susanne Kappesser, "'From the Seer to Be Seen': Wie Medialität und Blickkonstruktion in *Caché* Weißsein sichtbar machen," *Psychoanalyse und Filmtheorie* 12 (2016): 134–48, here 144; Brianne Gallagher, "Policing Paris: Private Publics and Architectural Media in Michael Haneke's *Caché*," *Journal for Cultural Research* 12.1 (2008): 19–38, here 22; Penney, "'You Never Look at Me from Where I See You,'" 79; Max Silverman, "The Empire Looks Back," *Screen* 48.2 (2007): 245–49, here 248; Laura Hubner, "Tension, Transition and Tone in Michael Haneke's *Caché*," *Studies in European Cinema* 9 (2012): 99–108, here 104; Kaul, *Michael Haneke*,

132; Celik, *In Permanent Crisis*, 66; C. L. Quinan, *Hybrid Anxieties: Queering the French-Algerian War and Its Postcolonial Legacies* (Lincoln: University of Nebraska Press, 2020), 72, 82–83. Recall Georges insinuating how Majid's parents got killed during the Paris massacre of October 17, 1961, how his parents adopted Majid, and how, out of jealousy, he told lies about Majid so as to have him sent off, which is exactly what happens—Majid will be sent to an orphanage. Undoubtedly, Georges's individual guilt does not consist in his lies as a child but in the adult's incapacity to respond to Majid and the fact that Majid has lived a life devoid of certain privileges Georges has enjoyed. Correspondingly, on the level of collective guilt, Haneke's film is not about France's committing of atrocities as colonizer per se but rather the refusal to deal with that legacy and the concomitant injustices that characterize the present day. Haneke explains in an interview how stunned he was when watching a documentary on the French-German television station ARTE about the Paris massacre of 1961, stunned not merely in light of the horrific event itself but the fact that it seemed excluded from public discourse: "I only learned of all this [...] by chance, in a documentary on ARTE concerning this event that occurred in 1961. And I was incredibly shocked, thinking, 'How can we have, in 1961, 200 corpses floating in the Seine, and nobody says anything about it for years and years? It irritated me to such an extent that I decided we must address it in this context" (Michael Haneke, interview by Serge Toubiana, DVD special feature on *Caché* [Culver City, CA: Sony Pictures Classics, 2006]; see also Michael Haneke, interview by Richard Porton, "Collective Guilt and Individual Responsibility," in *Michael Haneke: Interviews*, ed. Roy Grundmann, Fatima Naqvi, and Colin Root [Jackson: University Press of Mississippi, 2020], 78–82, here 78; Michael Haneke, interview by Katja Nicodemus and Thomas Assheuer, "Fear Is the Deepest Emotion," in *Michael Haneke: Interviews*, 83–89, here 83–84). The conclusion Haneke draws, namely, the applicability of this collective guilt to other countries and cultures, could, of course, be called into question, if only because such extrapolation seems at odds with the film's many narrative paradoxes, which resist generalization.

29 This emphasis on the watched in contrast to the watcher is what sets *Caché* most noticeably apart from surveillance classics such as Alfred Hitchcock's *Rear Window* (1954), Michelangelo Antonioni's *Blow-Up* (1966), and David Lynch's *Lost Highway* (1997).

30 On potential ways to differentiate between guilt and shame in *Caché*, see Joseph Vogl, "*Caché* (2005)," in *Filmische Moderne: 60 Fragmente*, ed. Oliver Fahle et al. (Bielefeld: Transcript, 2019), 365–70, here 369–70; Rowe, *Michael Haneke*, 165–72; Wheatley, *Michael Haneke's Cinema*, 164–66; Penney, "'You Never Look at Me from Where I See You,'" 89–93; Restuccia, "The Virtue of Blushing," 162–63.

31 See also Garrett Stewart, "Cimnemonics versus Digitime," in *Afterimages of Gilles Deleuze's Film Philosophy*, ed. D. N. Rodowick (Minneapolis: University of Minnesota Press, 2010), 327–50, here 349n32.

32 When Georges says, "It looks like a child's drawing," then of course he sees and perhaps knows something that Anne cannot see and know because the orbit of guilt within which Georges moves is one she does not intuit at this early point in the film ("I've no idea. I could not say"). Anne has no idea that what we see here is, at least partially, seen through George's inner eye, the internalized surveillance that inflects his each and every thought. On the efficacy of the drawings in *Caché*, see Guy Austin, "Drawing Trauma: Visual Testimony in *Caché* and *J'ai 8 ans*," *Screen* 48 (2007): 529–36; Nicholas Mirzoeff, *The Right to Look: A Counterhistory of Visuality* (Durham: Duke University Press, 2011), 258; Kaul, *Michael Haneke*, 132. See also Haneke, interview by Serge Toubiana.

33 The scene is symptomatic of Haneke's cinema in its emphasis on the status of the spectator: we assume the perspective of the dinner guests seated around the table, which look, along with Georges, at the television screen. This mise en abyme of the TV screen within the cinematic frame is again divided insofar as the image on the TV screen captures the perspective of a driver looking through the windshield of the car. On the ethical valences of spectatorship in Haneke's cinema, see Wheatley, *Michael Haneke's Cinema*, 153–87; Libby Saxton, "Close Encounters with Distant Suffering: Michael Haneke's Disarming Visions," in *Five Directors: Auteurism from Assayas to Ozon*, ed. Kate Ince (Manchester: Manchester University Press, 2008), 84–111; Rowe, *Michael Haneke*, 176–83; Walton, *Cinema's Baroque Flesh*, 67.

34 My discussion here reverberates with and is indebted to readings of *Caché* that—from distinct angles and with varying inflection—suggest a "merging" of the surveillance tapes and Georges's mental disposition over the course of the film. See, above all, Herzog, "The Banality of Surveillance," 33–36, here 34 and 36. See also Levin, "Five Tapes, Four Halls, Two Dreams," 81–84; Stewart, *Closed Circuits*, 164; Rowe, *Michael Haneke*, 186f., 190–91; Burris, "Surveillance and the Indifferent Gaze," 159, 161; Lie, *Towards a Political Aesthetics of Cinema*, 155, 161–64.

35 See also Kammerer, *Bilder der Überwachung*, 157–58, 320, 351.

36 Albeit less with regard to surveillance, Haneke's use of long takes has been at the center of a number of careful readings, including, above all, John David Rhodes, "The Spectacle of Skepticism: Haneke's Long Takes," in *On Michael Haneke*, ed. Price and Rhodes, 87–102. Cf. also Koepnick, *The Long Take*, 141–43.

37 Various critics have commented on the allegorical pull of the advertisement posters announcing the current movie performances of the 2004 season. See, for example, Stewart, *Framed Time*, 198–99; Herzog, "The Banality of Surveillance," 34; Lie, *Towards a Political Aesthetics of Cinema*, 162; Katharina Mueller, *Haneke: Keine Biografie* (Bielefeld: Transcript, 2014), 185; Ezra and Sillars, "*Hidden* in Plain Sight," 217. To be sure, we do not know which show Georges went to see, if any. But the fact that he seeks refuge in the movies is in itself a strong statement, not least regarding our focus on the issue of surveillance. For cinema does, of course, present a paradigmatic setup in terms of the asymmetrical dynamic of surveillance: we sit in the dark and look at a lit-up screen without allowing anyone to return the gaze. It is, not least, this anonymity that makes the cinematic experience so enticing. More concretely, we monitor Georges as he steps out of the movie theater into the dark and walks off to the right side of the frame. We observe him from a figurative position on the other side of the street that escapes his awareness, and at this point in the film, we certainly look at him as a suspect, as someone who warrants monitoring. It would appear that herein, indeed, lies our role as Haneke's cinematic spectators: we cannot simply lean back and enjoy the show but instead are put to work, are asked to look closely, like the guard in Bentham's prison tower. It is this surveillant dynamic that Haneke unremittingly translates into the cinematic setup, not in any static way (think: apparatus theory) but minutely enacted minute by minute, frame by frame (see also Libby Saxton, "Secrets and Revelations: Off-Screen Space in Michael Haneke's *Caché*," *Studies in French Cinema* 7.1 [2007]: 5–17, here 8; Janna Houwen, *Film and Intermediality: The Question of Medium Specificity in Contemporary Moving Images* [New York: Bloomsbury Academic, 2019], 265–68).

38 While on the surface this shot depicts a dream Georges has about his childhood, and while it seems motivated by his feelings of guilt associated with Majid, there is yet another orbit of guilt transpiring. For this rooster's life is one the director Haneke readily sacrifices for his film: Haneke was criticized for killing the animal for the sake of shooting the scene, an instrumental dismissal of nonhuman life that cloaks his actions under the very doom of guilt imbuing his story. See, for instance, Niels Niessen, "The Staged Realism of Michael Haneke's *Caché*," *Cinémas:*

Revue d'études cinématographiques/Journal of Film Studies 20.1 (2009): 181–99, here 196–97.

39 On the issue of intermediality in *Caché* in general and Haneke's relating of diegetic and extradiegetic space in particular, see Catherine Wheatley, *Caché (Hidden)* (London: British Film Institute, 2020), 73–75; Zimmer, *Surveillance Cinema*, 60–61; Levin, "Five Tapes, Four Halls, Two Dreams," 78–81; Christine Hanke, "[unsichtbar, verborgen, geheim]: Zur Reflexivität filmischer Bilder in Michael Hanekes *Caché*," in *Freeze Frames: Zum Verhältnis von Fotografie und Film*, ed. Stefanie Diekmann and Winfried Gerling (Bielefeld: Transcript, 2010), 131–45, here 140–44; Mattias Frey, "The Message and the Medium: Haneke's Film Theory and Digital Praxis," in *On Michael Haneke*, ed. Price and Rhodes, 153–65, here 162–63; Gilberto Perez, *The Eloquent Screen: A Rhetoric of Film* (Minneapolis: University of Minnesota Press, 2019), 312–14; Russell J. A. Kilbourn, *Cinema, Memory, Modernity: The Representation of Memory from the Art Film to Transnational Cinema* (New York: Routledge, 2010), 182, 187, 195; Vogl, "*Caché* (2005)," 368.

40 See also Ezra and Sillars, "*Hidden* in Plain Sight," 219. To be sure, Haneke's film defies being grasped by its constative economy—it develops its traction precisely in that murky space between narrative (the surveillance tapes, Georges's fears, his guilt) and Haneke's way of implicating us (into watching these tapes along with Georges, our repressed fears and guilty complicity). On the question of spectatorial complicity in Haneke, see Wheatley, *Michael Haneke's Cinema*, 153–87; Saxton, "Secrets and Revelations," 8 and 13; Seel, *The Arts of Cinema*, 122–24; Celik, *In Permanent Crisis*, 65–66 and 73–74; Fatima Naqvi, *Trügerische Vertrautheit: Filme von Michael Haneke* (Vienna: Synema, 2010), 22–23; Quinan, *Hybrid Anxieties*, 86; Camil Ungureanu, "Sacrifice, Violence and the Limits of Moral Representation in Haneke's *Caché*," in *Cinema and Sacrifice*, ed. Costica Bradatan and Camil Ungureanu (New York: Routledge, 2016), 53–65, here 61.

41 See, for example, Michael Haneke, interview by Norbert Creutz, "Je veux déstabiliser les gens," *Le Temps*, October 8, 2005. It goes without saying that Haneke as director of *Caché* does not escape the orbit of guilt himself. For a sensitive reading of how the filmmaker inscribes his presence in the film and, as such, implicates himself allegorically, see J. Macgregor Wise, *Surveillance and Film* (New York: Bloomsbury, 2016), 59; Herzog, "The Banality of Surveillance," 30; Perez, *The Eloquent Screen*, 312.

42 Walter Benjamin, *Gesammelte Schriften* (Frankfurt/M: Suhrkamp, 1985), 6: 92, qtd. in and here translated after Werner Hamacher, "Guilt History: Benjamin's Sketch 'Capitalism as Religion,'" trans. Kirk Wetters, *Diacritics* 32.3–4 (2002): 81–106, here 82–83. For a lucid discussion of the nexus between history and etiology, see Hamacher, 82–85. There is some reason to view surveillance in *Caché* as a form of control that shifts from Benthamite/Foucauldian disciplinary surveillance with a clear center of power (the watching guard) to a decentered Deleuzian conception of "societies of control" that entangle us as watched everywhere and ceaselessly (see Gogröf-Voorhees, "Surveillance and Voyerism," 264–78; Oliver C. Speck, "Self/Aggression: Violence in Films by Michael Haneke," *Modern Austrian Literature* 43 [2010]: 63–80, here 72; Araujo, "Inhospitality, Security, and the Global 'Homeland,'" 249; Gallagher, "Policing Paris," 19–38; cf. Foucault, *Discipline and Punish*, 195–228; and Deleuze, "Postscript on the Societies of Control," 3–7). Yet the critical dynamic of surveillance prevalent in the film harks back to the divine notion of God's ever-present gaze, a gaze that never sleeps and is mighty, ominous, or, as Georges says, "mysterious" because it does not allow itself to be localized or delineated and instead follows us everywhere and at all times ("Whither shall I go from thy spirit? or whither shall I flee from thy presence? / If I ascend up into heaven, thou art there: if I make my bed in hell, behold, thou art there"; Psalm 139:7–8).

Works Cited

Araujo, Susana. "Inhospitality, Security, and the Global 'Homeland' in Michael Haneke's *Caché*." In *Security and Hospitality in Literature and Culture: Modern and Contemporary Perspectives*, ed. Jeffrey Clapp and Emily Ridge, 243–57. New York: Routledge, 2016.

Austin, Guy. "Drawing Trauma: Visual Testimony in *Caché* and *J'ai 8 ans*." *Screen* 48 (2007): 529–36.

Bentham, Jeremy. *The Panopticon Writings*. London: Verso, 1995.

Böhme, Hartmut. *Natur und Subjekt*. Frankfurt/M: Suhrkamp Verlag, 1988.

Burris, Jennifer. "Surveillance and the Indifferent Gaze in Michael Haneke's *Caché*." *Studies in French Cinema* 11.2 (2011): 151–63.

Cazdyn, Eric. *The Already Dead: The New Time of Politics, Culture, and Illness*. Durham, NC: Duke University Press, 2012.

Celik, Ipek A. *In Permanent Crisis: Ethnicity in Contemporary European Media and Cinema*. Ann Arbor, MI: University of Michigan Press, 2015.

Chandna, Mohit. *Spatial Boundaries, Abounding Spaces: Colonial Borders in French and Francophone Literature and Film*. Leuven: Leuven University Press, 2021.

Chion, Michel. "Without Music: On *Caché*." In *A Companion to Michael Haneke*, ed. Roy Grundmann, 161–67. Malden, MA: Wiley-Blackwell, 2010.

Cowan, Michael. "Between the Street and the Apartment: Disturbing the Space of Fortress Europe in Michael Haneke." *Studies in European Cinema* 5.2 (2008): 117–29.

Crary, Jonathan. *24/7: Late Capitalism and the Ends of Sleep*. London: Verso, 2013.

Deleuze, Gilles. "Postscript on the Societies of Control." *October* 59 (1992): 3–7.

Dudai, Rina. "Trauma in Translation: Crossing the Boundaries between Psychoanalysis and Film." *Projections: The Journal for Movies and Mind* 8.1 (2014): 41–60.

Elsaesser, Thomas. "Performative Self-Contradictions: Michael Haneke's Mind Games." In *A Companion to Michael Haneke*, ed. Roy Grundmann, 53–74. Malden, MA: Wiley-Blackwell, 2010.

Ezra, Elizabeth, and Jane Sillars. "*Hidden* in Plain Sight: Bringing Terror Home." *Screen* 48.2 (2007): 215–21.

Farocki, Harun, dir. *Counter-Music*. Chicago, IL: Video Data Bank, 2004. DVD.

Foucault, Michel. *Discipline and Punish: The Birth of the Prison*. New York: Vintage Books, 1977.

Frey, Mattias. "The Message and the Medium: Haneke's Film Theory and Digital Praxis." In *On Michael Haneke*, ed. Brian Price and John David Rhodes, 153–65. Detroit, MI: Wayne State University Press, 2010.

Fussey, Pete, and Jon Coaffee. "Urban Spaces of Surveillance." In *Routledge Handbook of Surveillance Studies*, ed. Kirstie Ball et al., 201–8. New York: Routledge, 2012.

Gallagher, Brianne. "Policing Paris: Private Publics and Architectural Media in Michael Haneke's *Caché*." *Journal for Cultural Research* 12.1 (2008): 19–38.

Gavarini, Jehanne-Marie. "Rewind: The Will to Remember, the Will to Forget in Michael Haneke's *Caché*." In *Millennial Cinema: Memory in Global Film*, ed. Amresh Sinha and Terence McSweeney, 192–208. New York: Wallflower Press, 2011.

Gogröf-Voorhees, Andrea. "Surveillance and Voyeurism in Haneke's *Code Unknown* and *Caché*." In *Fascinatingly Disturbing: Interdisciplinary Perspectives on Michael Haneke's Cinema*, 259–81. Eugene, OR: Pickwick, 2010.

Grønstad, Asbjørn. *Screening the Unwatchable: Spaces of Negation in Post-Millennial Art Cinema*. London: Palgrave, 2012.

Haneke, Michael, dir. *Caché* (*Hidden*). 2004; Culver City, CA: Sony Pictures Home Entertainment, 2006. DVD.

Haneke, Michael. "Collective Guilt and Individual Responsibility." Interview by Richard Porton, in *Michael Haneke: Interviews*, ed. Roy Grundmann, Fatima Naqvi, and Colin Root, 78–82. Jackson, MS: University Press of Mississippi, 2020.

Haneke, Michael. "Fear Is the Deepest Emotion." Interview by Katja Nicodemus and Thomas Assheuer, in *Michael Haneke: Interviews*, ed. Roy Grundmann, Fatima Naqvi, and Colin Root, 83–89. Jackson, MS: University Press of Mississippi, 2020.

Haneke, Michael. "Je veux déstabiliser les gens." Interview by Norbert Creutz. *Le Temps*, October 8, 2005.

Hanke, Christine. "[unsichtbar, verborgen, geheim]: Zur Reflexivität filmischer Bilder in Michael Hanekes *Caché*." In *Freeze Frames: Zum Verhältnis von Fotografie und Film*, ed. Stefanie Diekmann and Winfried Gerling, 131–45. Bielefeld: Transcript, 2010.

Herzog, Todd. "The Banality of Surveillance: Michael Haneke's *Caché* and Life after the End of Privacy." *Modern Austrian Literature* 43.2 (2010): 25–40.

Houwen, Janna. *Film and Intermediality: The Question of Medium Specificity in Contemporary Moving Images*. New York: Bloomsbury Academic, 2019.

Hubner, Laura. "Tension, Transition and Tone in Michael Haneke's *Caché*." *Studies in European Cinema* 9 (2012): 99–108.

Humphreys, Stephen. "Conscience in the Datasphere." *Humanity* 6 (2015): 361–86.

Jorholt, Eva. "White Paranoia: Michael Haneke's *Caché* Reflected through Alain Robbe-Grillet's Novel *La Jalousie*." *Studies in French Cinema* 17 (2017): 91–108.

Kammerer, Dietmar. *Bilder der Überwachung*. Frankfurt/M: Suhrkamp, 2008.

Kappesser, Susanne. "'From the Seer to Be Seen': Wie Medialität und Blickkonstruktion in *Caché* Weißsein sichtbar machen." *Psychoanalyse und Filmtheorie* 12 (2016): 134–48.

Kaul, Susanne. *Michael Haneke: Einführung in seine Filme und Filmästhetik*. Paderborn: Wilhelm Fink Verlag, 2018.

Kilbourn, Russell J. A. *Cinema, Memory, Modernity: The Representation of Memory from the Art Film to Transnational Cinema*. New York: Routledge, 2010.

Kline, T. Jefferson. "The Intertextual and Discursive Origins of Terror in Michael Haneke's *Caché*." In *A Companion to Michael Haneke*, ed. Roy Grundmann, 551–61. Malden, MA: Wiley-Blackwell, 2010.

Koepnick, Lutz. *The Long Take: Art Cinema and the Wondrous*. Minneapolis, MN: University of Minnesota Press, 2017.

Landwehr, Margarete Johanna. "Voyeurism, Violence, and the Power of the Media: The Reader's/Spectator's Complicity in Jelinek's *The Piano Teacher* and Haneke's *La Pianiste, Caché, The White Ribbon*." *International Journal of Applied Psychoanalytic Studies* 8.2 (2011): 117–32.

Levin, Thomas Y. "Five Tapes, Four Halls, Two Dreams: Vicissitudes of Surveillant Narration in Michael Haneke's *Caché*." In *A Companion to Michael Haneke*, ed. Roy Grundmann, 75–90. Malden, MA: Wiley-Blackwell, 2010.

Lie, Sulgie. *Towards a Political Aesthetics of Cinema: The Outside of Film*. Amsterdam: Amsterdam University Press, 2020.

Lyon, David. *Surveillance Studies: An Overview*. Cambridge: Polity Press, 2007.

Manon, Hugh S. "Comment ça rien? Screening the Gaze in *Caché*." In *On Michael Haneke*, ed. Brian Price and John David Rhodes, 105–25. Detroit, MI: Wayne State University Press, 2010.

Mathiesen, Thomas. "The Viewer Society: Michel Foucault's Panopticon Revisited." *Theoretical Criminology* 1.2 (1997): 215–34.

McGill, Justice. "Bad Memories: Haneke with Locke on Personal Identity and Post-Colonial Guilt." *Film-Philosophy* 17.1 (2013): 134–53.

Mirzoeff, Nicholas. *The Right to Look: A Counterhistory of Visuality*. Durham, NC: Duke University Press, 2011.

Mueller, Katharina. *Haneke: Keine Biografie*. Bielefeld: Transcript, 2014.

Naqvi, Fatima. *Trügerische Vertrautheit: Filme von Michael Haneke*. Vienna: Synema, 2010.

Niessen, Niels. "The Staged Realism of Michael Haneke's *Caché*." *Cinémas: Revue d'études cinématographiques/Journal of Film Studies* 20.1 (2009): 181–99.

O'Donnell, Patrick. "Frame-Up: James, *Caché*, and the Borders of the Visible." *New Centennial Review* 13.2 (2013): 223–38.

Penney, James. "'You Never Look at Me from Where I See You': Postcolonial Guilt in *Caché*." *New Formations* 70 (2010): 77–93.

Perez, Gilberto. *The Eloquent Screen: A Rhetoric of Film*. Minneapolis, MN: University of Minnesota Press, 2019.

Quinan, C. L. *Hybrid Anxieties: Queering the French-Algerian War and Its Postcolonial Legacies*. Lincoln, NE: University of Nebraska Press, 2020.

Restuccia, Frances L. "The Virtue of Blushing: Assimilating Anxiety into Shame in Haneke's *Caché*." *Symplokē* 18 (2010): 155–70.

Rhodes, John David. "The Spectacle of Skepticism: Haneke's Long Takes." In *On Michael Haneke*, ed. Brian Price and John David Rhodes, 87–102. Detroit, MI: Wayne State University Press, 2010.

Rothberg, Michael. *Multidirectional Memory: Remembering the Holocaust in the Age of Decolonization*. Stanford, CA: Stanford University Press, 2009.

Rowe, Christopher. *Michael Haneke: The Intermedial Void*. Evanston, IL: Northwestern University Press, 2017.

Saxton, Libby. "Close Encounters with Distant Suffering: Michael Haneke's Disarming Visions." In *Five Directors: Auteurism from Assayas to Ozon*, ed. Kate Ince, 84–111. Manchester: Manchester University Press, 2008.

Saxton, Libby. "Secrets and Revelations: Off-Screen Space in Michael Haneke's *Caché*." *Studies in French Cinema* 7.1 (2007): 5–17.

Schiller, Friedrich. "The Song of the Bell." In *The Poems of Friedrich Schiller*, ed. and trans. E. P. Arnold-Foster, 246–59. New York: Henry Holt, 1902.

Schivelbusch, Wolfgang. *Disenchanted Night: The Industrialization of Light in the Nineteenth Century*. Berkeley, CA: University of California Press, 1995.

Seel, Martin. *The Arts of Cinema*. Ithaca, NY: Cornell University Press, 2018.

Silverman, Max. "The Empire Looks Back." *Screen* 48.2 (2007): 245–49.

Solomons, Jason. "We Love Hidden. But What Does It Mean?" *The Guardian*, February 18, 2006.

Speck, Oliver C. "Self/Aggression: Violence in Films by Michael Haneke." *Modern Austrian Literature* 43 (2010): 63–80.

Stewart, Garrett. "Cimnemonics versus Digitime." In *Afterimages of Gilles Deleuze's Film Philosophy*, ed. D. N. Rodowick, 327–50. Minneapolis, MN: University of Minnesota Press, 2010.

Stewart, Garrett. *Closed Circuits: Screening Narrative Surveillance*. Chicago, IL: University of Chicago Press, 2015.

Stewart, Garrett. *Framed Time: Toward a Postfilmic Cinema*. Chicago, IL: University of Chicago Press, 2007.
Stolleis, Michael. *The Eye of the Law: Two Essays on Legal History*. New York: Routledge, 2009.
Toubiana, Serge. Interview of Michael Haneke. Special feature, *Caché Hidden*, DVD. Culver City, CA: Sony Pictures Classics, 2006.
Ungureanu, Camil. "Sacrifice, Violence and the Limits of Moral Representation in Haneke's *Caché*." In *Cinema and Sacrifice*, ed. Costica Bradatan and Camil Ungureanu, 53–65. New York: Routledge, 2016.
Vogl, Joseph. "*Caché* 2005." In *Filmische Moderne: 60 Fragmente*, ed. Oliver Fahle et al., 365–70. Bielefeld: Transcript, 2019.
Walton, Saige. *Cinema's Baroque Flesh: Film, Phenomenology and the Art of Entanglement*. Amsterdam: Amsterdam University Press, 2016.
Wheatley, Catherine. *Caché (Hidden)*. London: British Film Institute, 2020.
Wheatley, Catherine. *Michael Haneke's Cinema: The Ethics of the Image*. New York: Berghahn Books, 2009.
Wise, J. Macgregor. *Surveillance and Film*. New York: Bloomsbury, 2016.
Zimmer, Catherine. *Surveillance Cinema*. New York: New York University Press, 2015.
Zureik, Elia. "Theorizing Surveillance: The Case of the Workplace." In *Surveillance as Social Sorting*, ed. David Lyon, 31–56. London: Routledge, 2003.

3 "In the Name of the Law"

Lang's *M*

I

Fritz Lang's classic 1931 film *M* invites us into its world via an overhead shot.[1] It conjures, at the outset, an all-seeing, quasi-divine perspective of a tenement backyard typical of Berlin. We see children standing in a circle and playing a game that invokes the child murderer, who keeps the city in suspense (Figure 3.1). Schematically, the circle itself is reminiscent of the divine symbol of God's eye, which sees all, evoking God's omniscience and omnipotence. When the Early Netherlandish painter Hieronymus Bosch, writes Astrit

Figure 3.1 *M* (Fritz Lang, 1931).

DOI: 10.4324/9781003229834-4

Schmidt-Burkhardt, in his famous painting *Seven Deadly Sins*, "inscribed the traditional symbol for divine omnipresence and omnipotence in the pure form of a circle, thus reducing it to an abstract figure, he created a lasting and impressive symbol for the unceasingly watchful eye of God."[2] From this biblical dimension of *super*vision or *sur*veillance, we hastily transition into a type of surveillance that conjures up the notion of "disciplinary society": these children practice the performance of internalized modes of behavior.[3] More specifically, they rehearse the implementation of established rules as to which child may remain in the circle and which is to be excluded. Of course, the game itself, strictly speaking, centers around a child murderer who has thrust the city into a state of crisis. But how this crisis is dealt with resonates, at least in its early stages, with the prototypical notion of a disciplinary society, in which the population is managed or rather is self-managing on the basis of rules and mores that regulate matters of social belonging and societal praxis.

Moments later we are presented with the child murderer himself, but only mediated by his shadow, which falls on the wanted poster regarding the search for him. In an attempt to lure his next victim, Beckert, the murderer, flatters little Elsie Beckmann as she walks home from school: "What a pretty ball you have there."[4] Tellingly, his posture is one of bending down to Elsie, feigning adult concern or care (Figure 3.2).

Figure 3.2 *M* (Fritz Lang, 1931).

Beckert finds opportunity for his deceptive maneuvers precisely in those spaces that remain unobserved by society. That this society, with its manifold disciplinary structures, sets out to guarantee the safety of the children, yet *fails* to do precisely that, transpires again and again. Consider, for example, the moment when the children are dismissed from *school*—the traditional institutional stronghold of disciplinary society. Or seconds later when a *police* officer escorts Elsie across the street in an effort to protect her from harm. Recall the low-angle shot of Mrs. Beckmann's neighbor at the beginning of the film as she—down from the balcony and equipped with a heavy laundry basket—admonishes the children to stop singing the "awful song";[5] or Mrs. Beckmann herself, the very epitome of *parental* surveillance, as she becomes increasingly worried and calls Elsie's name down the stairwell, out the window, and across the attic. She then directs her gaze at the empty chair where Elsie should now be sitting at lunch but is not—invoking her putative mischief. The fact that these various institutions of parental surveillance, police surveillance, school surveillance, and so forth *fail*—that the entire social order *fails*—becomes increasingly apparent and gives rise to a paradigm shift in the film.

II

In the wake of the failed panoptic surveillance, the child murderer puts the city in an atmospheric state of exception.[6] Not only the police but the entire city is mobilized to locate the child murderer,[7] who is affecting social life to the point of suspending all norms and usual procedures and who now must be tracked down. What conceptually emerges here is a transition from *panoptic* to *synoptic* surveillance—that is, we are no longer dealing with the surveillance of *many* by *one* (in Benthamite terms, of *many* prisoners by *one* guard), but increasingly with the surveillance of *one* person by *many* people.[8] The entire urban population is frantically searching for the child murderer. This incessantly heightened dynamic of synoptic surveillance is characterized by an increasing climate of "categorical suspicion."[9] We see, for instance, a crowd of people gathered on the street in front of an advertising column, reading a newspaper article about the most recent murder. The image cuts from the street to a small group of regular drinking mates in a bar who appear to be lifted straight from George Grosz's famous caricatures;[10] at the same time, the film's aural dimension establishes continuity in that they read and acoustically continue the same article as the people out in the street. "Anxiety among the general public is heightened by the police's failure to apprehend a suspect," we are told, and it seems precisely such heightened anxiety that serves as a catalyst of synoptic surveillance. While everybody appears to be in the grip of the latest news and wants to participate in hunting down the child murderer, people soon exhibit—typical for this form of synoptic surveillance—symptoms of distrust to the extent that everyone suspects everyone else. "Murderer!" one drinking brother says as he attacks another. "I'll see you in court!" the latter rebuffs. "I'll have you locked up!" the first one says, doubling down. "Slanderer! Trying to ruin my reputation," the altercation continues as they argue angrily. At first, Lang's enactment allows us to experience the heated altercation via a series of shot-reverse shots, but then he changes registers and uses a prolonged high-angle shot that implicates us as observers of the quarrel from a privileged position.

This divisive dynamic carries over into the next scene. "Damn slanderer! Besmirching a man's good name!" protests a resident whose house, seemingly for no good reason, is subjected to a police search. "A search warrant! [...] Searching a man's house based on an anonymous letter!" he fulminates. The point here is that the community, which is engendered and consolidated by the atmospheric state of exception, at the same time finds its normal structures and regulatory dynamics imperiled. How much communal customs and societal mores are unsettled and thrust into disarray is epitomized by the dismantling of friendships and neighborly relations and a general implosion of civility. Such societal disintegration similarly emerges when a markedly short pedestrian is approached by a little girl and asked for the time; their interaction instantly raises suspicion among pedestrians and results in the man's being questioned by a big, burly worker. Seconds later, the police, in the process of arresting a fare dodger, become involved. In a sheer hullabaloo, the fare dodger is suddenly suspected of being the child murderer. Symptomatic of this synoptic state of surveillance, the tracking and monitoring of the one, the child murderer, by the many, the mob, gives rise to an all-encompassing sense of distrust, a climate of categorical suspicion, which paralyzes communal life.

What appears particularly striking is how, on a macrosocial level, traditional divisions—such as those between law enforcement and lawbreaker, police and gangsters—are being suspended. An impressive cinematic enactment of this convergence transpires in the strategy meetings of the police and, respectively, of the gangsters, which Lang renders virtually indistinguishable, employing eloquent cross-cutting and corresponding mise-en-scènes so as to present them as one, seemingly jointly concerted, initiative. Sentences and gestures begun by members of one group are continued by members of the other, cigarette smoke ceaselessly clouds the images of both settings, and in dramatic terms both sessions move toward a state of utter exhaustion for everyone. Both police and gangsters set out to find the child murderer, albeit their approaches are decidedly different. The police's surveillance efforts can be characterized as scientifically oriented if one considers,[11] for example, the meticulous analysis of fingerprints (Figure 3.3), an unmistakable allusion to the early twentieth-century emergence of dactyloscopy.[12]

Figure 3.3 *M* (Fritz Lang, 1931).

Recall the painstaking exactitude with which Beckert's handwriting is scrutinized, an instance of the now-debunked pseudoscience of graphology, which Lang's film seems to parodize. Consider the methodical review of files of patients released from mental institutions in view of the question whether the child murderer might be among them—a compelling example of file-based surveillance rendered possible by an extensive bureaucratic apparatus.[13] Notice, finally, how Inspector Lohmann reviews the identification card of each visitor at a bar known to be frequented by the city's racketeers and hoodlums—yet another very systematic mode of identification and tracking.[14]

The film takes an altogether different approach to the gangsters, who do everything they can to incessantly keep an eye on the entire city. As the leader of the gangsters, Schränker, stresses, "Every square mile must be under constant surveillance. No child in this city must take a single step without us knowing it." It is the beggars who allow for the realization of this plan, for they are in the "privileged" position of being ubiquitous without being noticed. They are part of the city's infrastructure, an integral component that is not consciously registered as such, and therefore offer the best opportunity to see without being seen. Thus, the beggars are recruited by the criminals, unequivocally invoking the spirit of Brecht's 1928 *Threepenny Opera*.[15] The "organization of beggars" has its "members" cover every street corner, from which they can observe and communicate every suspicious occurrence.[16] Complete cartographic assessment of the city, as well as its staffing with control personnel, are intended to achieve what their technological equivalent in the late twentieth century, closed-circuit television (CCTV), was able to do.[17]

Reflecting on these different methods of surveillance, the scientifically inflected approach of the police, on the one hand, and, on the other, the more flexible and situational approach of the criminals, who view the child murderer as detrimental to their illicit business dealings given the police's heightened alertness, one cannot help but notice a certain transition. Consider the surveillance strategy of the police:

> I'm quite certain that information on the individual in question must already exist somewhere. Being the severely pathological case that he is, he has no doubt already had some kind of contact with the authorities. *That's why all health care facilities, prisons, clinics and insane asylums must be encouraged to cooperate with us unequivocally.* We specifically need information on those released after being deemed harmless to society but who, due to their inclinations, could be the murderer.[18]

The traditional institutions of disciplinary surveillance are, as it were, amalgamated and embedded here into a network.[19] Schränker, the leader of the criminals, employs this notion of the network explicitly: "We must cover the city with a *net of informers*. Every square foot must be under permanent control. [...] It must be people who can go anywhere without causing a stir, follow anyone without attracting attention, follow any child to any house without arousing any suspicion."[20] In the context of this network of informers embodied by the beggars, any information or suspicion can be passed on seamlessly. Classic forms of surveillance, such as an observer with binoculars hiding behind curtains, familiar from so many surveillance films, appear obsolete (Figure 3.4). Instead, control systems such as the "new type of control clock"[21] that secures the office building in which Beckert is hiding and which is directly connected to the police station are becoming increasingly prevalent. Lang's film shows us the control clock and then inserts the close-up of a "general diagram" that illustrates its rhizomatic operating structure (Figure 3.5).[22] What emerges might be described as a *transition* from a centralized arrangement of power to a decentralized one. When describing this transition from institutions to networks topologically, one might speak of a shift from a *vertical* structure (the prison guards who monitor the inmates) to a *horizontal* design. The vertical system is increasingly replaced by a flat

Figure 3.4 *M* (Fritz Lang, 1931).

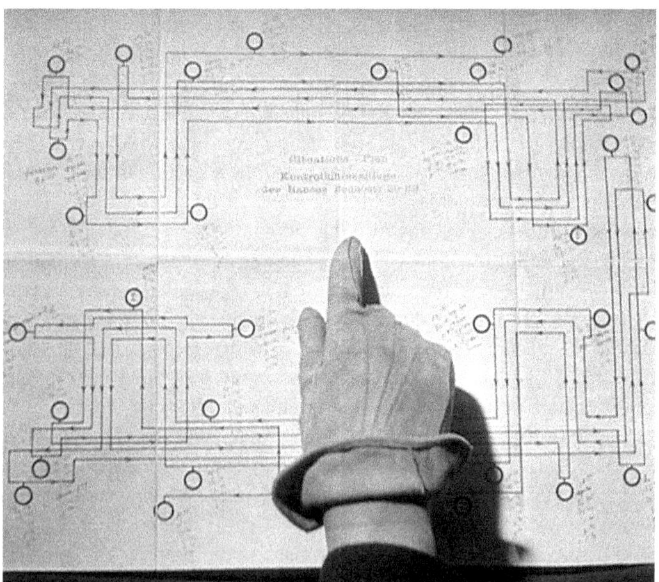

Figure 3.5 *M* (Fritz Lang, 1931).

formation in which there is no longer a concentric consolidation of power directed at subordinate subjects or "docile bodies," as Foucault described it for institutions in disciplinary societies.[23] Instead, we are dealing with a network architecture in which everyone is involved, where control is both carried out and experienced by everyone; that is, everyone is watcher and watched at the same time.[24]

III

It goes without saying that surveillance takes place not only on a diegetic level; surveillance is not merely a matter of the police or the gangsters and their recruits, the beggars. Lang's camera itself is *surveillant* in various ways. At times, we witness the typical affectless camera gaze that nowadays is associated with automated camera surveillance and that indifferently records events or objects—think of the seemingly photographic stills in Mrs. Beckmann's apartment, or the stoic panning shot displaying the confiscated items of a police raid. Next to these affectless and matter-of-fact shots, testifying to the film's New Objectivity inflection,[25] we encounter moments in which a (at times shaky) camera appears prying, inquisitive, displaying a curiosity that seems strangely furtive. What is more, we in our role as spectators are unremittingly implicated in the experience of surveillance. Recall the very first scene in which we assume a quasi-divine perspective on the tenement backyard with its circularly configured group of children, mirroring the parental surveillance of the mother watching over and after the children from the balcony up high.[26] Consider the memorable scene in which Beckert stands in front of a shop window and looks at the displayed knives arranged as a rhombus. Suddenly he notices a little girl in the reflection of the window and feels overcome by his demonic desire to lay hands on the child, but the next moment the girl is taken into her mother's arms, eluding the imminent danger. Beckert has to calm himself and downs two cognacs on the patio of a restaurant, hidden behind vines (Figure 3.6). Curiously, we observe the scene through the eye of the animated camera, that camera that, by way of a tracking shot, sneaks up to the hedge, monitors Beckert clandestinely, and then, as he gets up, abruptly tracks back so as to avoid being caught in the act of surveillance.[27] That is, the dynamic of seeing without being seen is unmistakably enacted by the camera and allows us to perceive surveillance as something not solely conceptually posited but indeed performed. And importantly, this performance or enactment emphatically involves us, in that we, perforce, must participate in the experience of surveillance.

Another example presents itself when the beggars find Beckert and mark him with an "M"—the letter "M," which seems prefigured by the lines on the human palm and is now with chalk applied to Beckert's shoulder. The girl, doomed to be his next victim, points out, "Mister. […] You got some white

Figure 3.6 *M* (Fritz Lang, 1931).

stuff on your coat." Beckert turns around and sees the mark in a mirror; he recognizes himself as the murderer in the reflection, then frightens, and in a certain way identifies that other state of his personality, which he speaks of in front of the kangaroo court toward the end of the film. Beckert's disturbing confrontation with his murderous alter ego, which tracks and violates little girls, is translated into an image here. Lang visually enacts Beckert's split personality or, more technically, his dissociative identity disorder. Immediately following the self-recognition and the concomitant trepidation, Beckert stares directly into the camera—thereby breaking the fourth wall—as if knowing that he is being observed *by us*. And we are startled and likely feel caught as observers.[28] In other words, again we encounter that allegorical enactment of surveillance in which surveillance is not merely asserted thematically but rather conjured up as an experience in which we participate.

Surveillance runs through the film all the way to the eventual kangaroo court scene, where Beckert is put on "trial" and given the opportunity to expound on his actions. His exposition refers to an "evil thing"[29] inside him that coerces him to "do it"—"Don't want to! Must! Don't want to! Must!" Notably, Beckert's compulsion to murder incessantly gives rise to a form of self-observation or self-surveillance ("And then a voice cries out"), but it is doomed to succumb to the stronger demonic drive ("and I can't listen anymore"). Put differently, Beckert unmistakably struggles with the "bestial" urges that coerce him to murder; he fights an internal adversary—and yet always fails. His pleading gaze directly into the camera—again breaking the fourth wall—indicates how much we, as observers, are thrust into the role of judges before whom Beckert is trying to make his case.

Against the background of the link established at the beginning between surveillance and the divine, it is noteworthy that here, at the end of the film, surveillance is set in relation to evil. To be sure, Beckert is an enemy of society and is fought accordingly by the police and gangsters. However, his characterization as an enemy takes an extreme form, as becomes particularly clear in Schränker's words: "[W]e must draw a firm line between ourselves and this man they're looking for! [...] [T]his monster has no right to survive! He must be killed, eliminated, exterminated! Without mercy or compassion!" Beckert is, in the words of Carl Schmitt, not simply an *enemy* in the sense of a "legitimate" political adversary, but a *foe*, "whom one must fight to the death and destroy."[30] Throughout the film, and especially during the "trial" scene, such dehumanization occurs again and again; Beckert is characterized as a "monster" that "must be extinguished like a bonfire," that "must be obliterated, wiped out." The defense counsel's insistence on the rights that Beckert is entitled to as a "human being" is dismissed because he is precisely *not* viewed as a "human being" ("Kill the monster!" "Put the animal to death!" "Annihilate the monster!" "That's not a human being"). This dehumanization prepares and putatively legitimizes the lynching or "death penalty" planned for Beckert.[31] And it is precisely his existence as the extraneous Other outside any notion of society that also seems to have inspired the anti-Semitic appropriation in Fritz Hippler's 1940 film *The Eternal Jew*, in which the child murderer Beckert and the "Jew Lorre," who portrays him, appear interchangeable.[32]

IV

While we are able to identify a failure of disciplinary forms of surveillance in the course of *M*, the film's finale gives rise to their putative reinstatement. The police, apprised by the defected criminal Franz, storm the cellar of the abandoned distillery, where the collected gangsters surrender to them with their arms raised. A hand falls on Beckert's shoulder, and from off-screen, we hear: "In the name of the law." Cut. A somewhat unmotivated epilogue begins, "In the name of the people," establishing a link to the preceding scene. We see a panel of judges, barricaded behind legal tomes—once more conjuring up the nexus between surveillance and bureaucracy—deliver a verdict regarding Beckert "in the name of the people." That this form of society with its traditional structures has fallen out of time can be inferred when the three mothers—in the middle, Elsie Beckmann's mother—lament, "This will not bring our children back." To be sure, these are mothers who have fallen short in providing parental supervision. But they also intuit the inadequacy of the state's methods of surveillance or supervision, which are alluded to here unconvincingly. A new age is on the horizon, that of the decentralized, horizontally organized society, which Fritz Lang's *M* in a certain way spells out, or at least prefigures.

For the time being, the synoptic state of surveillance, in which police and gangsters fight alongside each other, evaporates. Everything is back to normal; the criminals are viewed as opponents by the police and are doomed to be arrested. The police appear in their weakness as the supposedly authoritarian force, the "eye of the law," they claim to be—but they no longer really are.[33] They are hardly present in the film, and in the end not at all, and this nonpresence is of course synonymous with the nonpresence of their effectiveness, of their ability to successfully surveil and monitor. By the end of the film, the temporary decentering and horizontalization, the shift from institutions to networks, from corporeality to functionality, seems thwarted. The emergence of a societal state in which surveillance is exercised and experienced by everyone—the collapse of the dichotomy between watchers and watched, leading to a conflation of both—appears foiled. This becomes evident as the police storm the cellar and then, even more emphatically, in the epilogue, where the fading disciplinary forces appear once again in their unequivocal claim to validity. The fact that Lang's film does not simply display this faltering of the opposition between watchers and watched and its subsequent reinstatement, but instead allows us to experience it through our involvement as constant observers, renders *M*, in the best sense of the term, an instance of surveillance cinema.

Notes

1 *M*, directed by Fritz Lang (1931; New York: Criterion, 2004), DVD. Unless otherwise noted, translations follow the subtitles of this print.

2 Astrit Schmidt-Burkhardt, "The All-Seer: God's Eye as Proto-Surveillance," in *Ctrl Space: Rhetorics of Surveillance from Bentham to Big Brother*, ed. Thomas Levin, Ursula Frohne, and Peter Weibel (Cambridge, MA: MIT Press, 2002), 17–31, here 20. Quite differently, and perhaps less compellingly in our context, Siegfried Kracauer, in his analysis of Lang's *Dr. Mabuse, the Gambler,* sees the symbol of the circle as evoking a "state of chaos" (*From Caligari to Hitler* [Princeton: Princeton University Press, 2004], 83).

3 On the notion of disciplinary society, see, above all, Michel Foucault, *Discipline and Punish: The Birth of the Prison* (New York: Vintage Books, 1977), 135–228.

4 For Michel Chion's reading of this scene in light of his influential theorization of acousmatic sound, understood as "sound that is heard without its [...] source being seen," see Chion, *The Voice in Cinema* (New York: Columbia University Press, 1999), 15–57, here 18–19. On the nexus between acousmatic sound and surveillance, see Chion, 24–27.

5 Maria Tatar has offered an extremely thoughtful analysis that pays heed to the film's maternal politics and its "subterranean 'female' regime of surveillance." In contrast to Tatar's discussion of the opening scene as evoking an "element of arbitrary selection," the "role of random" and "haphazard" selection, my reading seeks

to emphasize the importance of disciplinary order and control in the children's game that aims precisely at taming these random forces. Hence the crucial role of "repetition" in the game, hence its "ritualistic" character. See Maria Tatar, *Lustmord: Sexual Murder in Weimar Germany* (Princeton: Princeton University Press, 1995), 153–72, here 170 and 166.

6 The concept of the "state of exception" (*Ausnahmezustand*), which Carl Schmitt popularized in its legal connotation, is employed here in a broader sense, focusing on the sociopsychological ramifications. See Carl Schmitt, *Political Theology: Four Chapters on the Concept of Sovereignty*, trans. George Schwab (Chicago: University of Chicago Press, 2006), especially chapter 1.

7 On the efficacy of this mobilization in *M*, see Anton Kaes, "The Cold Gaze: Notes on Mobilization and Modernity," *New German Critique* 59 (1993): 105–17; and Kaes, *M* (London: Bloomsbury, 2021), 52–70.

8 As for the etymology of the term "synopticism," it is "composed of the Greek word *syn* which stands for 'together' or 'at the same time,' and *opticon*, which [...] has to do with the visual." I employ the concept of synoptic surveillance from sociologist Thomas Mathiesen's important article "The Viewer Society: Michel Foucault's Panopticon Revisited." Mathiesen probes "one limited and consciously selected aspect of Michel Foucault's use of Jeremy Bentham's concept of the 'Panopticon': in his book *Discipline and Punish*, the aspect of surveillance, and the emphasis on a fundamental change and break which presumably occurred in the 1800s from social and theatrical arrangements, where the many saw the few, to modern surveillance activities where the few see the many." Mathiesen argues "that Foucault contributes in an important way to our understanding of and sensitivity regarding modern surveillance systems and practices, which are expanding at an accelerating rate, but that he overlooks an opposite process of great significance which has occurred simultaneously and at an equally accelerated rate." While the Foucauldian panopticon permits the few to watch the many, Mathiesen's notion of the "synopticon," epitomized markedly by the mass media, particularly television, empowers "the many [...] to see [...] the few." To be sure, the two concepts are not to be viewed in oppositional terms but rather as "reciprocal functions," as Mathiesen himself emphasizes ("The Viewer Society: Michel Foucault's Panopticon Revisited," *Theoretical Criminology* 1.2 [1997]: 215–34, here 219 and 215).

9 Gary T. Marx, "Undercover in Contemporary Perspective: Some Implications for Knowledge and Social Research," in *Undercover: Police Surveillance in Comparative Perspective*, ed. Cyrille Fijnaut and Gary T. Marx (The Hague: Kluwer Law International, 1995), 323–37, here 336; Gary T. Marx, *Undercover: Police Surveillance in America* (Berkeley: University of California Press, 1988), 206–33, here 219. Adopting a phrase by Onora O'Neill, David Lyon, in a related context, speaks of an "enhanced culture of suspicion." See David Lyon, "9/11, Synopticon, and Scopophilia: Watching and Being Watched," in *The New Politics of Surveillance and Visibility*, ed. Kevin D. Haggerty and Richard V. Ericson (Toronto: University of Toronto Press, 2006), 35–54, here 38.

10 On Grosz's resonance with Lang's *M*, see Kaes, *M*, 54; and Tom Gunning, *The Films of Fritz Lang: Allegories of Vision and Modernity* (London: BFI Publishing, 2000), 176.

11 On the scientific investigation methods of the police, see also Kata Gellen, "Indexing Identity: Fritz Lang's *M*," *Modernism/modernity* 22.3 (2015): 425–48, here 428; and Todd Herzog, *Crime Stories: Criminalistic Fantasy and the Culture of Crisis in Weimar Germany* (New York: Berghahn Books, 2009), 127. Jacques Rancière offers a circumspect discussion of how "maps and magnifying glasses, inventories and drag-nets trap the murderer," in *Film Fables* (New York: Berg, 2006), 16, 18, 48–53, here 18.

12 On the significance of Alphonse Bertillon's anthropometric approach in criminal history and its eventual replacement by dactyloscopy, see Jonathan Finn, *Capturing the Criminal Image: From Mug Shot to Surveillance Society* (Minneapolis: University of Minnesota Press, 2009), 1–56; and Btihaj Ajana, *Governing through Biometrics: The Biopolitics of Identity* (New York: Palgrave Macmillan, 2013), 27–29.

13 See, above all, Max Weber, *Economy and Society: An Outline of Interpretive Sociology* (Berkeley: University of California Press, 1978). See also Christopher Dandeker, *Surveillance, Power and Modernity: Bureaucracy and Discipline from 1700 to the Present Day* (Cambridge: Polity Press, 1990); and David Lyon, *Surveillance Studies: An Overview* (Cambridge: Polity Press, 2007), 79–83.

14 See Valentin Groebner, *Who Are You? Identification, Deception, and Surveillance in Early Modern Europe* (New York: Zone Books, 2007), especially 12, 171–221, and 229. See also Rex Ferguson, Melissa M. Littlefield, and James Purdon, "Introduction," in *The Art of Identification: Forensics, Surveillance, Identity*, ed. Ferguson, Littlefield, and Purdon (University Park: The Pennsylvania State University Press, 2021), 1–20.

15 In an interview with Gero Gandert, Lang underscored the Brechtian influence on his film (see Gero Gandert, "Fritz Lang on *M*: An Interview," in *Fritz Lang: Interviews*, ed. Barry Keith Grant [Jackson: University of Mississippi Press, 2003], 33–37, here 35). For a careful discussion of the impact of Brecht's Epic Theater and his *Threepenny Opera* on *M*, see Kaes, *M*, 34–37 and 48–51. On certain "Brechtian effects" in *M*, see also Patrick McGilligan, *Fritz Lang: The Nature of the Beast* (Minneapolis: University of Minnesota Press, 2013), here 156.

16 Once the beggars locate Beckert, the news is immediately communicated by telephone to the gangsters' command center, and only here does the sophistication of the surveillance methods of the criminals and, respectively, the beggars they have recruited become clear. The auditory pursuit of the murderer ("His whistling gave him away") results in his visual marking ("They put a mark on him"), and from here on the noose on Beckert slowly tightens: "They're following the mark. He isn't out of sight for a second." The communication between commando leadership and the personnel on the street is reminiscent of the carefully composed opening scene of Lang's 1922 *Dr. Mabuse, the Gambler* as far as its communicative efficacy across disparate spaces is concerned. As Beckert's "every move is being watched," we follow the minutely orchestrated system of beggars coordinating with each other, all working toward one goal, the capture of the murderer. For a shrewd reading of the role of (tele)communication in the opening scene of Lang's *Dr. Mabuse, the Gambler*, see Gunning, *The Films of Fritz Lang*, 94–99.

17 On the relation between surveillance, urbanity, and modes of spatialization, see Alan Reeve, "Exercising Control at the Urban Scale: Towards a Theory of Spatial Organisation and Surveillance," in *Surveillance, Architecture and Control: Discourses on Spatial Culture*, ed. Susan Flynn and Antonia Mackay (London: Palgrave Macmillan, 2019), 19–56. Of course, surveillance in urban spaces almost inevitably precipitates, in the words of Michel de Certeau, "contradictory movements that counter-balance and combine themselves outside the reach of panoptic power. [...] Beneath the discourses that ideologize the city, the ruses and combinations of powers that have no readable identity proliferate; without points where one can take hold of them, without rational transparency, they are impossible to administer." Consequently, de Certeau calls for an analysis of the "microbe-like, singular and plural practices which an urbanistic system was supposed to administer or suppress [...]; one can follow the swarming activity of these procedures that, far from being regulated or eliminated by panoptic administration, have reinforced themselves in a proliferating illegitimacy, developed and insinuated themselves into the networks of surveillance, and combined in

accord with unreadable [...] tactics" (*The Practice of Everyday Life* [Berkeley: University of California Press, 1984], 95–96). For a perceptive update on the matter, see Clive Norris, "The Success of Failure: Accounting for the Global Growth of CCTV," in *Routledge Handbook of Surveillance Studies*, ed. Kirstie Ball, Kevin D. Haggerty, and David Lyon (New York: Routledge, 2012), 251–58. See also Mark Andrejevic, "Automated Surveillance," in *Routledge Handbook of Digital Media and Communication*, ed. Leah A. Lievrouw and Brian D. Loader (New York: Routledge, 2021), 242–53.

18 Emphasis mine. In contrast to this complete interplay between and utter interweaving of various institutions, Foucault writes: "Discipline [...] requires *enclosure*, the specification of a place heterogeneous to all others and closed in upon itself. It is the protected place of disciplinary monotony" (*Discipline and Punish*, 141).

19 In his elliptical "Postscript on the Societies of Control," Gilles Deleuze famously notes: "Foucault located the *disciplinary societies* in the eighteenth and nineteenth centuries; they reach their height at the outset of the twentieth. They initiate the organization of vast spaces of enclosure." In contrast to Foucault's analysis of disciplinary societies and their characteristic "environments of enclosure," Deleuze contends: "We are in a generalized crisis in relation to all the environments of enclosure—prison, hospital, factory, school, family." Deleuze goes so far as to predict the "replacement" of disciplinary societies with "societies of control" and offers the following enigmatic image: "Enclosures are *molds*, distinct castings, but controls are a *modulation*, like a self-deforming cast that will continuously change from one moment to the other, or like a sieve whose mesh will transmute from point to point" (3–4). Deleuze associates the emergence of control societies with the—increasingly computerized—second half of the twentieth century. While Fritz Lang's *M* can hardly be considered an illustration of a control society, one may find that it anticipates moments of it, as it were, *avant la lettre*. See Deleuze, "Postscript on the Societies of Control," *October* 59 (1992): 3–7, here 3–4.

20 Translation modified.

21 Translation modified.

22 We see a security guard of the office building doing his work, systematically setting the control clocks. Just as he passes the door behind which Beckert is hiding, Beckert *listens* intently, all while trying to remain *unheard*—one of the many inconspicuous but ubiquitous moments of surveillance in Lang's cinematic oeuvre, which includes, not least, *auditory* surveillance in its asymmetrical logic of hearing without being heard. Cf. Dörte Zbikowski, "The Listening Ear: Phenomena of Acoustic Surveillance," in *Ctrl Space*, ed. Levin, Frohne, and Weibel, 33–49.

23 Foucault, *Discipline and Punish*, 135.

24 See also Byung-Chul Han's conception of the "*aperspectival* panopticon" where the "distinction between center and periphery, which is fundamental to the Benthamian panopticon, has disappeared" (*The Transparency Society* [Stanford: Stanford University Press, 2015], 45).

25 Garrett Stewart has eloquently commented on the matter-of-fact quality of these shots and their repercussions with the New Objectivity movement. See Garrett Stewart, "Frame-Advance Modernism: The Case of Fritz Lang's *M*," in *Moving Modernisms: Motion, Technology, and Modernity*, ed. David Bradshaw, Laura Marcus, and Rebecca Roach (Oxford: Oxford University Press, 2016), 236–56. Cf. also Garrett Stewart, *Closed Circuits: Screening Narrative Surveillance* (Chicago: University of Chicago Press, 2015), 22–59.

26 The discourse of parental surveillance permeates the film literally from the first scene (tenement backyard scene) to the last (three mothers scene). To my knowledge, Maria Tatar is the only critic to date to have delved into the film's multifarious politics of parental surveillance in detail. See Tatar, *Lustmord*, 153–72.

27 See also Kaes, *M*, 61; and Gunning, *The Films of Fritz Lang*, 185–86. On the camera's becoming "more and more an accomplice in a system of surveillance, total record-keeping and even paranoia," see, moreover, Sabine Müller, "Embodied Cognition and Camera Mobility in F. W. Murnau's *The Last Laugh* and Fritz Lang's *M*," *Paragraph* 37.1 (2014): 32–46, here 43.

28 For a nuanced, albeit differently calibrated, reading of this scene, see Stewart, *Closed Circuits*, 44 and 46.

29 Translation modified. On the notion of evil, see Alain Badiou, *Ethics: An Essay on the Understanding of Evil* (New York: Verso, 2002); and Jean Baudrillard, *The Transparency of Evil: Essays on Extreme Phenomena* (New York: Verso, 1993).

30 Carl Schmitt, the notorious and perhaps most intriguing thinker on the issue of enmity, distinguishes between "real" and "absolute" enmity: While the real enemy, in the words of translator G. L. Ulmen, is regarded as "a legitimate opponent, whom one fights according to recognized rules," the absolute enemy or "foe" is a "lawless opponent, whom one must fight to the death and destroy" (*Theory of the Partisan: Intermediate Commentary on the Concept of the Political* [New York: Telos Press, 2007], 89–90). When dealing with absolute enmity, writes Schmitt, one "degrades the enemy into moral or other categories and is forced to make of him a monster that not only must be defeated, but also destroyed" (92–93n93). In various ways, Beckert echoes Schmitt's notion of the absolute enemy or foe, not least in his being characterized as "inhuman" (94). As thought-provoking as Schmitt's distinction may be, its dichotomous structure inevitably remains incommensurable with Lang's poetic work, its visual complexities, and poetic impasses.

31 "To confiscate the word humanity, to invoke and monopolize such a term probably has certain incalculable effects, such as denying the enemy the quality of being human and declaring him to be an outlaw of humanity," Schmitt writes (*The Concept of the Political* [Chicago: University of Chicago Press, 2007], 54).

32 On the reception of Lang's *M* during the Nazi era, see Todd Herzog, "Fritz Lang's *M*: An Open Case," in *Weimar Cinema: An Essential Guide to Classic Films of the Era*, ed. Noah Isenberg (New York: Columbia University Press, 2009), 291–309, here 305–7. For a highly perceptive discussion of *M* vis-à-vis discourses of medical surveillance, see Paul Dobryden, "Marked Man: Fantasies of the Able Body in Fritz Lang's *M*," *German Studies Review* 45.2 (2022): 407–28, here especially 417–24.

33 The metaphor of "eye of the law" typically "refers to the police, who are protecting the citizens from crime, 'watching' while they sleep. […] The citizen's sleep is protected by the well-ordered state, its law, and a police force committed to warding off danger and guaranteeing safety" (Michael Stolleis, *The Eye of the Law: Two Essays on Legal History* [New York: Routledge, 2009], 1–2). To be sure, just as God's gaze denotes "care" and "control," so the police's status as secular equivalent of God's gaze is importantly ambiguous (Lyon, *Surveillance Studies*, 3; Dietmar Kammerer, *Bilder der Überwachung* [Frankfurt/M: Suhrkamp, 2008], 104–5, 227–31). Against this backdrop, it is unsurprising that Beckert shuns the controlling authority of the police throughout most the film, yet when faced with the prospect of being lynched by the underworld mob he insists on his right to be handed over to the police, thereby invoking their protective responsibility toward the citizenry: "I demand to be handed over to the police!" On the polyvalent connotation of the divine gaze, see also David Lyon, "Surveillance and the Eye of God," *Studies in Christian Ethics* 27.1 (2014): 21–32; regarding the equivocal metaphor of the "eye of the law" as epitomized by the police, see also Stolleis, *The Eye of the Law*, 5–7.

Works Cited

Ajana, Btihaj. *Governing through Biometrics: The Biopolitics of Identity*. New York: Palgrave Macmillan, 2013.

Andrejevic, Mark. "Automated Surveillance." In *Routledge Handbook of Digital Media and Communication*, ed. Leah A. Lievrouw and Brian D. Loader, 242–53. New York: Routledge, 2021.

Badiou, Alain. *Ethics: An Essay on the Understanding of Evil*. New York: Verso, 2002.

Baudrillard, Jean. *The Transparency of Evil: Essays on Extreme Phenomena*. New York: Verso, 1993.

Chion, Michel. *The Voice in Cinema*. New York: Columbia University Press, 1999.

Dandeker, Christopher. *Surveillance, Power and Modernity: Bureaucracy and Discipline from 1700 to the Present Day*. Cambridge: Polity Press, 1990.

de Certeau, Michel. *The Practice of Everyday Life*. Berkeley, CA: University of California Press, 1984.

Deleuze, Gilles. "Postscript on the Societies of Control." *October* 59 (1992): 3–7.

Dobryden, Paul. "Marked Man: Fantasies of the Able Body in Fritz Lang's *M*." *German Studies Review* 45.2 (2022): 407–28.

Ferguson, Rex, Melissa M. Littlefield, and James Purdon. "Introduction." In *The Art of Identification: Forensics, Surveillance, Identity*, ed. Rex Ferguson, Melissa M. Littlefield, and James Purdon, 1–20. University Park, PA: Pennsylvania State University Press, 2021.

Finn, Jonathan. *Capturing the Criminal Image: From Mug Shot to Surveillance Society*. Minneapolis, MN: University of Minnesota Press, 2009.

Foucault, Michel. *Discipline and Punish: The Birth of the Prison*. New York: Vintage Books, 1977.

Gandert, Gero. "Fritz Lang on *M*: An Interview." In *Fritz Lang: Interviews*, ed. Barry Keith Grant, 33–37. Jackson: University of Mississippi Press, 2003.

Gellen, Kata. "Indexing Identity: Fritz Lang's *M*." *Modernism/modernity* 22.3 (2015): 425–48.

Groebner, Valentin. *Who Are You? Identification, Deception, and Surveillance in Early Modern Europe*. New York: Zone Books, 2007.

Gunning, Tom. *The Films of Fritz Lang: Allegories of Vision and Modernity*. London: BFI Publishing, 2000.

Han, Byung-Chul. *The Transparency Society*. Stanford, CA: Stanford University Press, 2015.

Herzog, Todd. *Crime Stories: Criminalistic Fantasy and the Culture of Crisis in Weimar Germany*. New York: Berghahn Books, 2009.

Herzog, Todd. "Fritz Lang's *M*: An Open Case." In *Weimar Cinema: An Essential Guide to Classic Films of the Era*, ed. Noah Isenberg, 291–309. New York: Columbia University Press, 2009.

Kaes, Anton. "The Cold Gaze: Notes on Mobilization and Modernity." *New German Critique* 59 (1993): 105–17.

Kaes, Anton. *M*. London: Bloomsbury, 2021.

Kammerer, Dietmar. *Bilder der Überwachung*. Frankfurt/M: Suhrkamp, 2008.

Kracauer, Siegfried. *From Caligari to Hitler*. Princeton, NJ: Princeton University Press, 2004.

Lang, Fritz, dir. *M*. 1931; New York: Criterion, 2004. DVD.

Lyon, David. "9/11, Synopticon, and Scopophilia: Watching and Being Watched." In *The New Politics of Surveillance and Visibility*, ed. Kevin D. Haggerty and Richard V. Ericson, 35–54. Toronto: University of Toronto Press, 2006.

Lyon, David. "Surveillance and the Eye of God." *Studies in Christian Ethics* 27.1 (2014): 21–32.

Lyon, David. *Surveillance Studies: An Overview*. Cambridge: Polity Press, 2007.

Marx, Gary T. *Undercover: Police Surveillance in America*. Berkeley, CA: University of California Press, 1988.

Marx, Gary T. "Undercover in Contemporary Perspective: Some Implications for Knowledge and Social Research." In *Undercover: Police Surveillance in Comparative Perspective*, ed. Cyrille Fijnaut and Gary T. Marx, 323–37. The Hague: Kluwer Law International, 1995.

Mathiesen, Thomas. "The Viewer Society: Michel Foucault's Panopticon Revisited." *Theoretical Criminology* 1.2 (1997): 215–34.

McGilligan, Patrick. *Fritz Lang: The Nature of the Beast*. Minneapolis, MN: University of Minnesota Press, 2013.

Müller, Sabine. "Embodied Cognition and Camera Mobility in F. W. Murnau's *The Last Laugh* and Fritz Lang's *M*." *Paragraph* 37.1 (2014): 32–46.

Norris, Clive. "The Success of Failure: Accounting for the Global Growth of CCTV." In *Routledge Handbook of Surveillance Studies*, ed. Kirstie Ball, Kevin D. Haggerty, and David Lyon, 251–58. New York: Routledge, 2012.

Rancière, Jacques. *Film Fables*. New York: Berg, 2006.

Reeve, Alan. "Exercising Control at the Urban Scale: Towards a Theory of Spatial Organisation and Surveillance." In *Surveillance, Architecture and Control: Discourses on Spatial Culture*, ed. Susan Flynn and Antonia Mackay, 19–56. London: Palgrave Macmillan, 2019.

Schmidt-Burkhardt, Astrit. "The All-Seer: God's Eye as Proto-Surveillance." In *Ctrl Space: Rhetorics of Surveillance from Bentham to Big Brother*, ed. Thomas Levin, Ursula Frohne, and Peter Weibel, 17–31. Cambridge, MA: MIT Press, 2002.

Schmitt, Carl. *The Concept of the Political*. Chicago, IL: University of Chicago Press, 2007.

Schmitt, Carl. *Political Theology: Four Chapters on the Concept of Sovereignty*. Trans. George Schwab. Chicago, IL: University of Chicago Press, 2006.

Schmitt, Carl. *Theory of the Partisan: Intermediate Commentary on the Concept of the Political*. New York: Telos Press, 2007.

Stewart, Garrett. *Closed Circuits: Screening Narrative Surveillance*. Chicago, IL: University of Chicago Press, 2015.

Stewart, Garrett. "Frame-Advance Modernism: The Case of Fritz Lang's *M*." In *Moving Modernisms: Motion, Technology, and Modernity*, ed. David Bradshaw, Laura Marcus, and Rebecca Roach, 236–56. Oxford: Oxford University Press, 2016.

Stolleis, Michael. *The Eye of the Law: Two Essays on Legal History*. New York: Routledge, 2009.

Tatar, Maria. *Lustmord: Sexual Murder in Weimar Germany*. Princeton, NJ: Princeton University Press, 1995.

Weber, Max. *Economy and Society: An Outline of Interpretive Sociology*. Berkeley, CA: University of California Press, 1978.

Zbikowski, Dörte. "The Listening Ear: Phenomena of Acoustic Surveillance." In *Ctrl Space: Rhetorics of Surveillance from Bentham to Big Brother*, ed. Thomas Levin, Ursula Frohne, and Peter Weibel, 33–49. Cambridge, MA: MIT Press, 2002.

Index

Notes: Page numbers followed by 'n' denote notes.

For Product Safety Concerns and Information please contact our EU
representative GPSR@taylorandfrancis.com
Taylor & Francis Verlag GmbH, Kaufingerstraße 24, 80331 München, Germany

www.ingramcontent.com/pod-product-compliance
Lightning Source LLC
LaVergne TN
LVHW010939110826
845149LV00013B/2670
* 9 7 8 1 0 3 2 1 3 5 5 6 4 *